E S T A T E   P U B I   T I O N S

EASTBOURNE

LEWES   HAILSHAM   BEXHILL

CW00344908

8 HAILSHAM **9**	

LEWES	
4	**5**

BEXHILL	
24	**25**

23

Cooden

6 **7** Seaford	

Polegate
10   **11**   **14**   **15**   Pevensey

12   **13**   Pevensey Bay

Willingdon   Langney
16   **17** **18**   **19**

Hampden Park

Meads

20   **22** **21**

EASTBOURNE

ROAD MAP   Pages 2–3

ENLARGED CENTRE   Page 22

INDEX TO STREETS   Page 26

Every effort has been made to verify
the accuracy of information in this
book but the publishers cannot accept
responsibility for expense or loss
caused by an error or omission.
Information that will be of assistance
to the user of the maps will be welcomed.

The representation on these maps of a
road, track or path is no evidence of the
existence of a right of way.

Car Park	🅿
Public Convenience	🄲
Place of Worship	✚
One-way Street	→
Pedestrianized	▨
Post Office	●

Scale of street plans 4 inches to 1 mile
Unless otherwise stated

Street plans prepared and published by ESTATE PUBLICATIONS, Bridewell House, TENTERDEN, KENT.
The Publishers acknowledge the co-operation of the local authorities
of towns represented in this atlas.

© Crown Copyright 2001   All rights reserved
© Estate Publications 566 C   ISBN 1 84192 092 4   Licence number 100019031

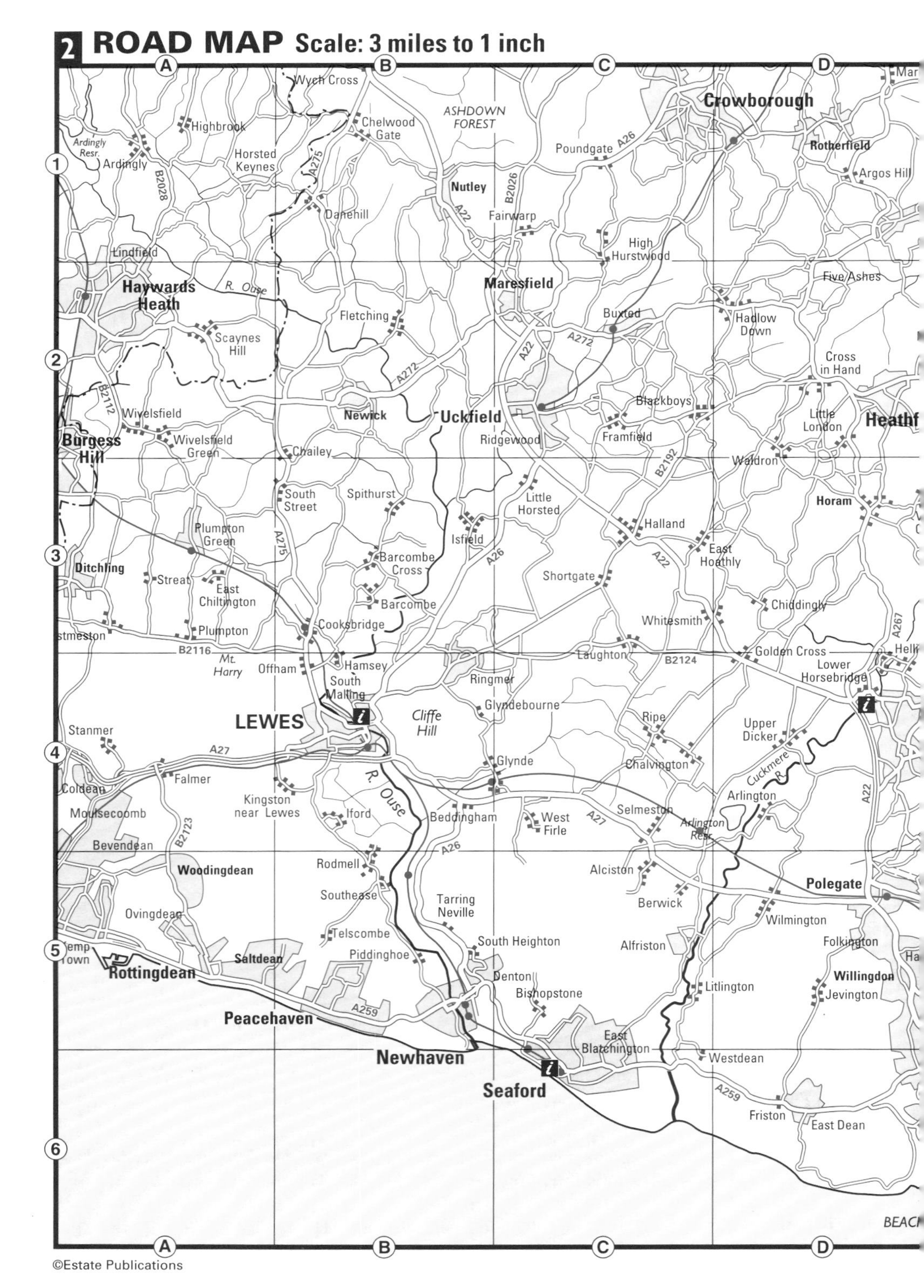
2
ROAD MAP Scale: 3 miles to 1 inch
A
B
C
D
1
2
3
4
5
6
Wych Cross
Highbrook
Chelwood Gate
ASHDOWN FOREST
Crowborough
Ardingly Resr.
Ardingly
Horsted Keynes
B2028
A275
Nutley
B2026
Poundgate
A26
Rotherfield
Argos Hill
Danehill
A22
Fairwarp
Lindfield
High Hurstwood
Haywards Heath
R. Ouse
Maresfield
Five Ashes
Fletching
Buxted
Hadlow Down
Scaynes Hill
A272
Cross in Hand
B2112
Wivelsfield
Newick
Uckfield
Blackboys
Little London
Heathf
Burgess Hill
Wivelsfield Green
Ridgewood
Framfield
Chailey
Waldron
B2192
South Street
Spithurst
Little Horsted
Horam
Plumpton Green
Halland
Isfield
Ditchling
East Hoathly
Barcombe Cross
Streat
Shortgate
East Chiltington
Barcombe
Chiddingly
Whitesmith
Cooksbridge
A267
stmeston
Plumpton
B2116
Mt. Harry
Offham
Hamsey
Laughton
B2124
Golden Cross
Lower Horsebridge
South Malling
Ringmer
Glyndebourne
Cliffe Hill
LEWES
Stanmer
Ripe
Upper Dicker
A27
Glynde
Chalvington
Coldean
Falmer
Cuckmere R.
Arlington
Moulsecoomb
Kingston near Lewes
Iford
R. Ouse
Beddingham
West Firle
Selmeston
Arlington Resr.
Bevendean
B2123
A26
Rodmell
Alciston
Woodingdean
Polegate
Southease
Berwick
Tarring Neville
Ovingdean
Wilmington
Telscombe
South Heighton
Alfriston
Folkington
Kemp Town
Saltdean
Piddinghoe
Rottingdean
Denton
Willingdon
Bishopstone
Litlington
Jevington
Peacehaven
A259
East Blatchington
Westdean
Newhaven
Seaford
Friston
East Dean
BEACH
©Estate Publications

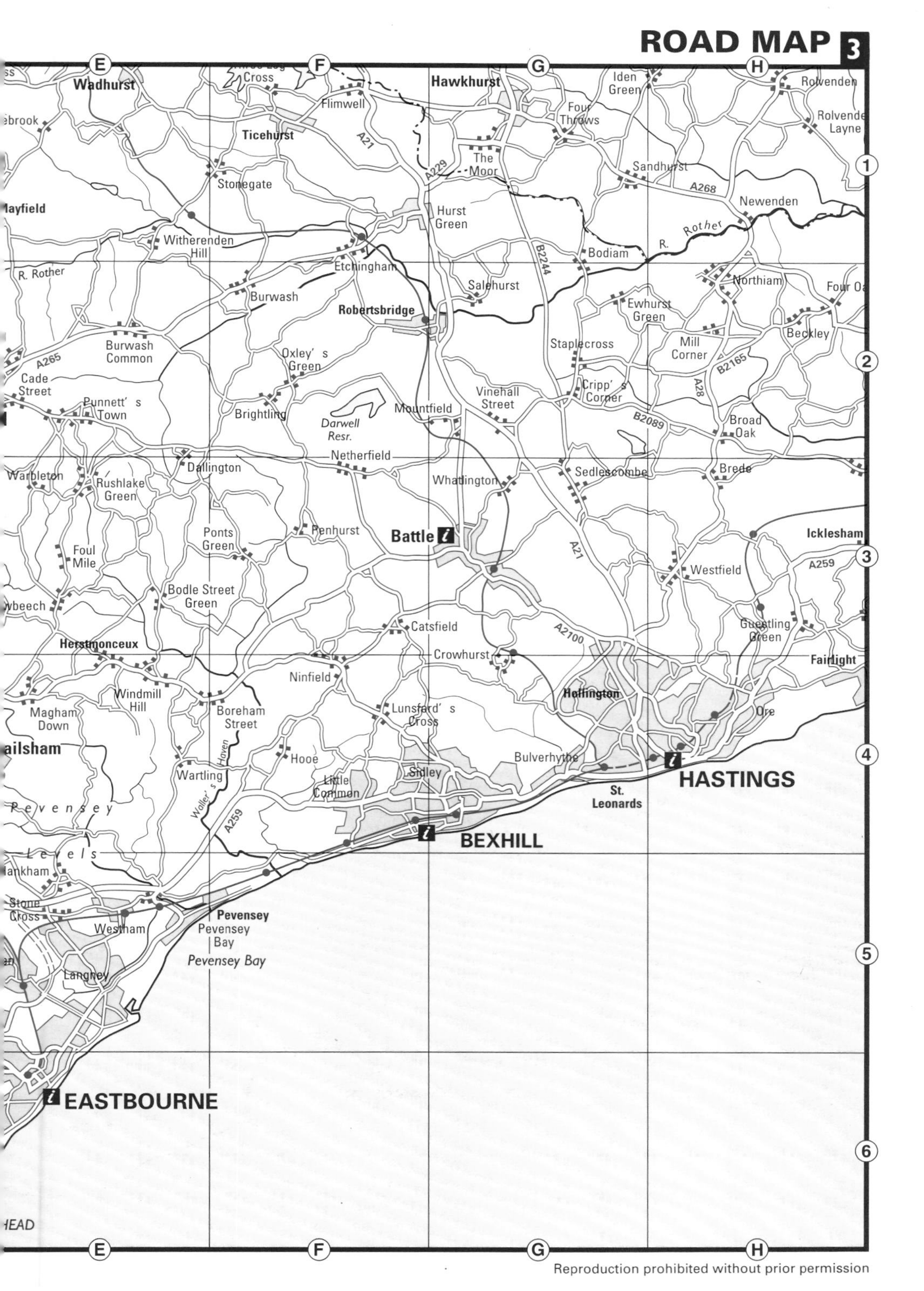
Wadhurst
Flimwell
Hawkhurst
Iden Green
Rolvenden
Rolvenden Layne
Four Throws
Ticehurst
A21
The Moor
A229
Sandhurst
A268
Newenden
Stonegate
Mayfield
Hurst Green
Witherenden Hill
Etchingham
R. Rother
Bodiam
B2244
R. Rother
Northiam
Salehurst
Burwash
Robertsbridge
Ewhurst Green
Four Oaks
Beckley
Burwash Common
Staplecross
Mill Corner
A265
Cade Street
Oxley's Green
B2165
Punnett's Town
Brightling
Darwell Resr.
Mountfield
Vinehall Street
Cripp's Corner
A28
B2089
Broad Oak
Netherfield
Warbleton
Dallington
Whatlington
Sedlescombe
Brede
Rushlake Green
Penhurst
Battle
Icklesham
Ponts Green
Foul Mile
A21
Westfield
A259
Bodle Street Green
Catsfield
A2100
Guestling Green
Herstmonceux
Crowhurst
Fairlight
Ninfield
Windmill Hill
Hollington
Magham Down
Boreham Street
Lunsford's Cross
Ore
Hailsham
Hooe
Waller's Haven
Bulverhythe
Wartling
Sidley
Little Common
St. Leonards
HASTINGS
Pevensey
A259
BEXHILL
Levels
Hankham
Stone Cross
Pevensey
Westham
Pevensey Bay
Pevensey Bay
Langney
EASTBOURNE
E
F
G
H
1
2
3
4
5
6

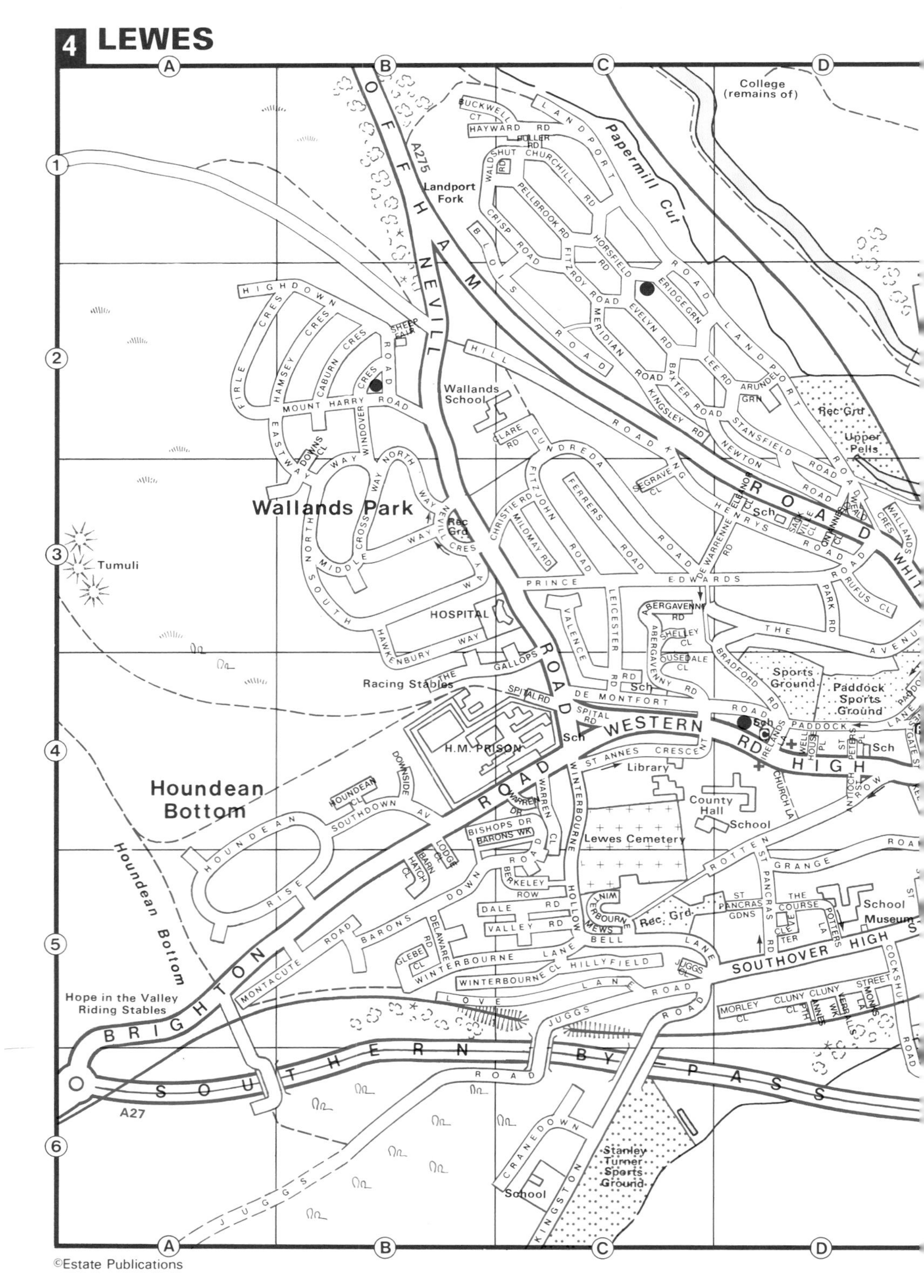
4
LEWES
A
B
C
D
1
2
3
4
5
6
College (remains of)
Papermill Cut
OFFHAM
A275
Landport Fork
BUCKWELL CT
HAYWARD RD
FULLER RD
WALDSHUT RD
CHURCHILL RD
LANDPORT ROAD
PELLBROOK RD
CRISP ROAD
BLOIS ROAD
HORSFIELD RD
FITZROY ROAD
ERIDGE GRN
EVELYN RD
MERIDIAN ROAD
BAXTER ROAD
LEE RD
ARUNDEL GRN
KINGSLEY RD
STANSFIELD ROAD
NEWTON ROAD
Rec Grd
Upper Pells
HIGHDOWN CRES
HAMSEY CRES
CABURN CRES
SHEEP FAIR
FIRLE CRES
MOUNT HARRY ROAD
NEVILL ROAD
HILL ROAD
KING HENRYS ROAD
Wallands School
CLARE RD
GUNDREDA RD
SEGRAVE CL
EASTWAY
DOWNS CL
WINDOVER CRES
NORTH WAY
Wallands Park
NEVILL CRES
CROSS WAY
NORTH WAY
MIDDLE WAY
SOUTH WAY
Rec Grd
CHRISTIE RD
FITZJOHN RD
MILDMAY RD
FERRERS ROAD
ELEANOR CL
Sch
SACKVILLE CL
ST ANNES CL
WEALD
WALLANDS CRES
WHITE
DE WARRENNE RD
PRINCE EDWARDS ROAD
RUFUS CL
PARK RD
Tumuli
HOSPITAL
HAWKENBURY WAY
VALENCE RD
LEICESTER RD
ABERGAVENNY RD
SHELLEY CL
OUSEDALE CL
BRADFORD RD
THE AVENUE
Sports Ground
Paddock Sports Ground
THE GALLOPS
Racing Stables
SPITAL RD
DE MONTFORT ROAD
Sch
PADDOCK LANE
H.M. PRISON
WESTERN RD
Sch
HIGH
IRELANDS LA
WELL HOUSE PL
ST PETERS PL
GATE ST
Sch
ST ANNES CRESCENT
Library
CHURCH LA
ANTIOCH ST
ROW
County Hall
School
Houndean Bottom
DOWNSIDE
HOUNDEAN CL
SOUTHDOWN AV
HOUNDEAN RISE
WARREN DR
WARREN CL
WINTERBOURNE HOLLOW
BISHOPS DR
BARONS WK
LODGE CL
BARN HATCH CL
BERKELEY ROW
Lewes Cemetery
ROTTEN ROW
ST PANCRAS RD
GRANGE ROAD
THE COURSE
School
Museum
ST PANCRAS GDNS
Rec. Grd
DALE RD
VALLEY RD
WINTERBOURNE MEWS
BELL LANE
CLEVE TER
POTTERS LA
SOUTHOVER HIGH ST
COCKSHUT ROAD
Houndean Bottom
BARONS DOWN ROAD
MONTACUTE ROAD
DELAWARE RD
GLEBE CL
WINTERBOURNE LANE
WINTERBOURNE CL
HILLYFIELD
JUGGS CL
WINTERBOURNE LANE
JUGGS ROAD
LOVE LANE
MORLEY CL
CLUNY ST
CLUNY PTH
ANNES PTH
VERRALLS WK
MONKS LA
Hope in the Valley Riding Stables
BRIGHTON ROAD
SOUTHERN BY-PASS
A27
ROAD
CRANEDOWN
KINGSTON ROAD
School
Stanley Turner Sports Ground
JUGGS ROAD
©Estate Publications

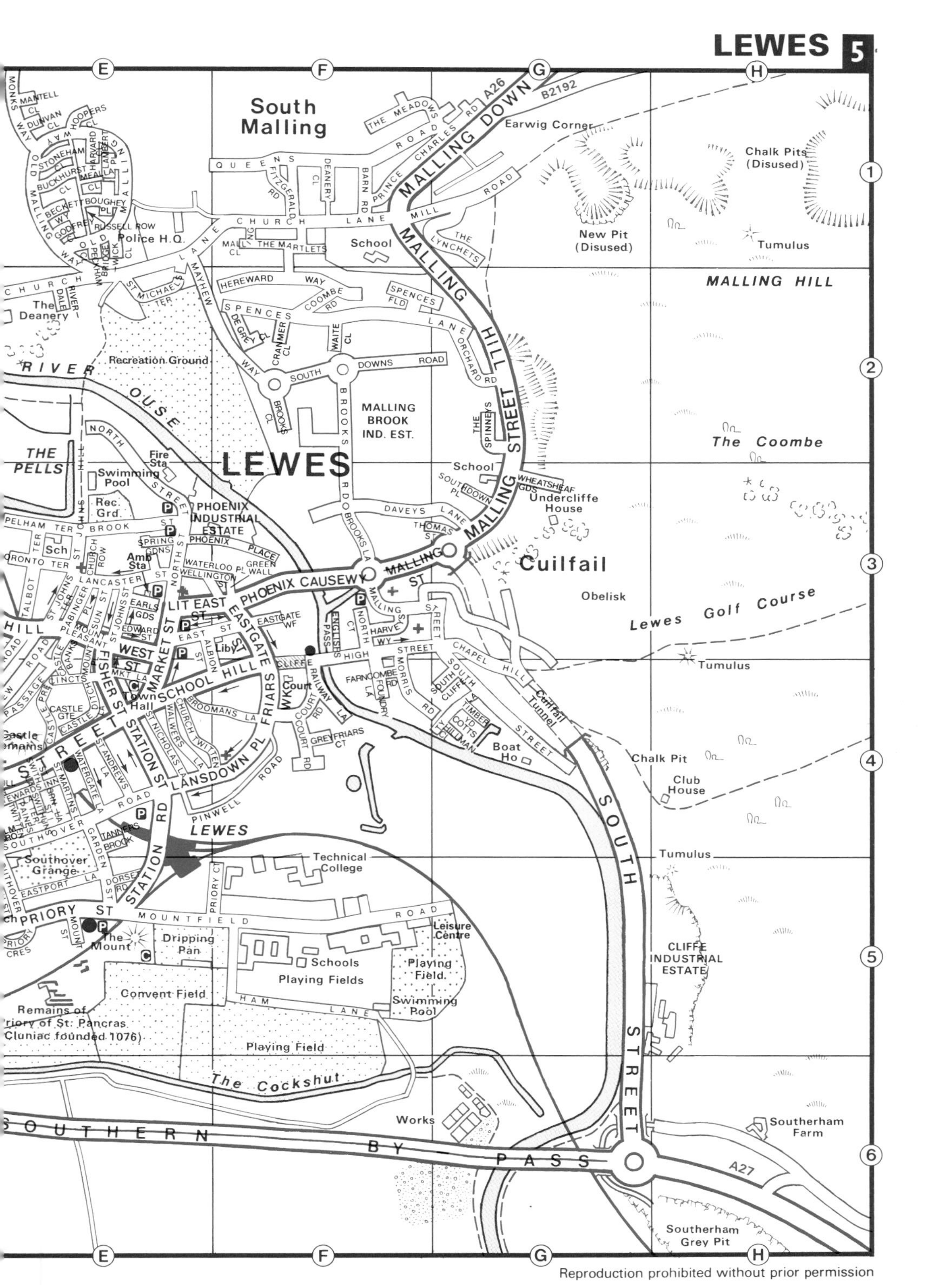
South Malling
LEWES
Cuilfail
MALLING HILL
The Coombe
Chalk Pits (Disused)
New Pit (Disused)
Tumulus
Earwig Corner
A26
B2192
MALLING DOWN
MALLING HILL
MALLING STREET
MALLING ST
CHURCH LANE
QUEENS RD
FITZGERALD RD
DEANERY CL
BARN RD
PRINCE CHARLES RD
THE MEADOWS ROAD
MILL ROAD
THE LYNCHETS
THE MARTLETS
School
Police H.Q.
RUSSELL ROW
MONKS WAY
MANTELL CL
DUNVAN CL
HOOPERS CL
STONEHAM CL
BUCKHURST CL
HARVARD CL
LAMBERT PL
MEAL CL
BECKETT WY
BOUGHEY PL
GODFREY CL
OLD MALLING WAY
BRIDGE WICK CL
PEXHAM
The Deanery
RIVER DALE
ST MICHAELS TER
HEREWARD WAY
COOMBE RD
SPENCES FLD
SPENCES LANE
DE GREY CL
CRANMER CL
WAITE CL
MAYHEW WAY
SOUTH DOWNS ROAD
BROOKS CL
BROOKS RD
ORCHARD RD
MALLING BROOK IND. EST.
THE SPINNEYS
Recreation Ground
RIVER OUSE
THE PELLS
NORTH STREET
Fire Sta
Swimming Pool
Rec. Grd.
PHOENIX INDUSTRIAL ESTATE
PHOENIX PLACE
PHOENIX CAUSEWAY
SOUTHDOWN PL
WHEATSHEAF GDS
Undercliffe House
DAVEYS LANE
THOMAS ST
BROOKS LA
PELHAM TER
BROOK ST
SPRING GDNS
Sch
Amb Sta
WATERLOO PL
GREEN WALL
WELLINGTON ST
LANCASTER ST
EARLS GDS
EDWARD ST
LIT EAST ST
EAST ST
EASTGATE ST
EASTGATE WF
ALBION ST
Liby
MARKET ST
WEST ST
MKT LA
FISHER ST
Town Hall
SCHOOL HILL
BROOMANS LA
CHURCH TWITTEN
WALWERS LA
ST NICHOLAS LA
STATION ST
FRIARS WK
Court
COURT RD
GREYFRIARS CT
RAILWAY LA
ENGLISH PASS
NORTH CT
HARVEY WY
CLIFFE HIGH STREET
FARNCOMBE LA
FOUNDRY
MORRIS RD
SOUTH ST
SOUTH CLIFFE
TIMBER YD COTTS
HILLMAN CL
CHAPEL HILL
Cuilfail Tunnel
Boat Ho
Obelisk
Lewes Golf Course
Chalk Pit
Club House
Castle Remains
CASTLE GTE
CASTLE PRECINCTS
CASTLE DITCH LA
ST ANDREWS LA
ST MARTINS LA
WATERGATE LA
LANSDOWN PL
PINWELL ROAD
LEWES
STATION RD
TANNERS BROOK
SOUTHOVER ROAD
Southover Grange
GARDEN ST
DORSET RD
EASTPORT LA
PRIORY ST
PRIORY CRES
MOUNT
The Mount
Technical College
PRIORY CT
MOUNTFIELD ROAD
Leisure Centre
Dripping Pan
Schools
Playing Fields
Playing Field
Convent Field
HAM LANE
Swimming Pool
Remains of Priory of St. Pancras (Cluniac founded 1076)
The Cockshut
Works
SOUTHERN BY PASS
SOUTH STREET
CLIFFE INDUSTRIAL ESTATE
Southerham Farm
A27
Southerham Grey Pit
E
F
G
H
1
2
3
4
5
6

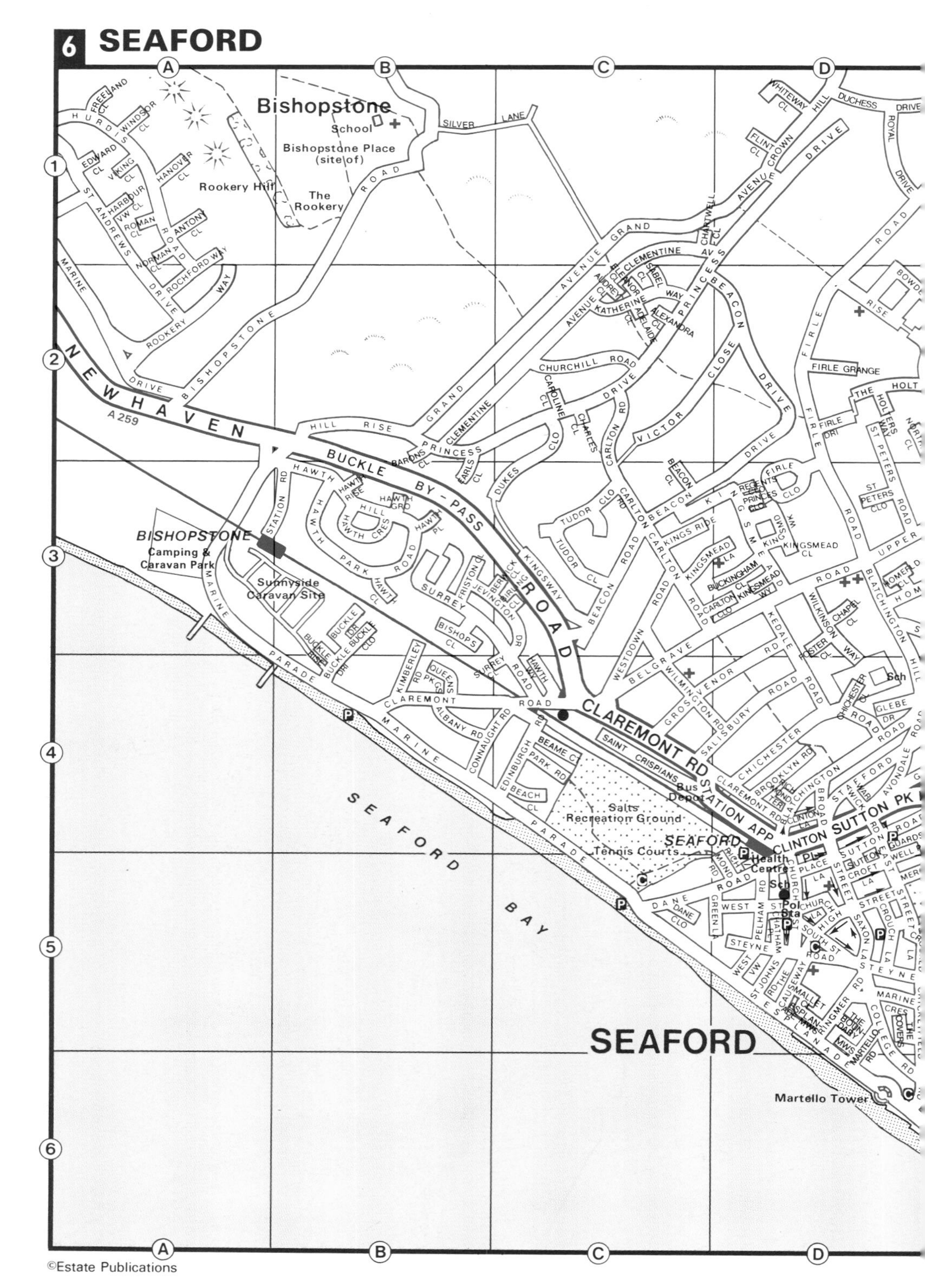
6
SEAFORD
Bishopstone
School
Bishopstone Place
(site of)
Rookery Hill
The
Rookery
SILVER LANE
BISHOPSTONE ROAD
NEWHAVEN ROAD
A 259
BUCKLE BY-PASS
GRAND AVENUE
PRINCESS DRIVE
BEACON DRIVE
VICTOR CLOSE
CHURCHILL ROAD
CARLTON ROAD
KINGSWAY
KINGSMEAD
HAWTH PARK ROAD
STATION RD
BISHOPSTONE
Camping &
Caravan Park
Sunnyside
Caravan Site
MARINE PARADE
CLAREMONT ROAD
CLAREMONT RD
SAINT CRISPIANS
STATION APP
Bus
Depot
Salts
Recreation Ground
Tennis Courts
SEAFORD
Health
Centre
Sch
Pol
Sta
CLINTON PL
SUTTON PK
BROAD STREET
CHURCH ST
HIGH ST
SOUTH ST
STEYNE ROAD
DANE ROAD
BLATCHINGTON ROAD
FIRLE ROAD
SEAFORD BAY
SEAFORD
Martello Tower
©Estate Publications

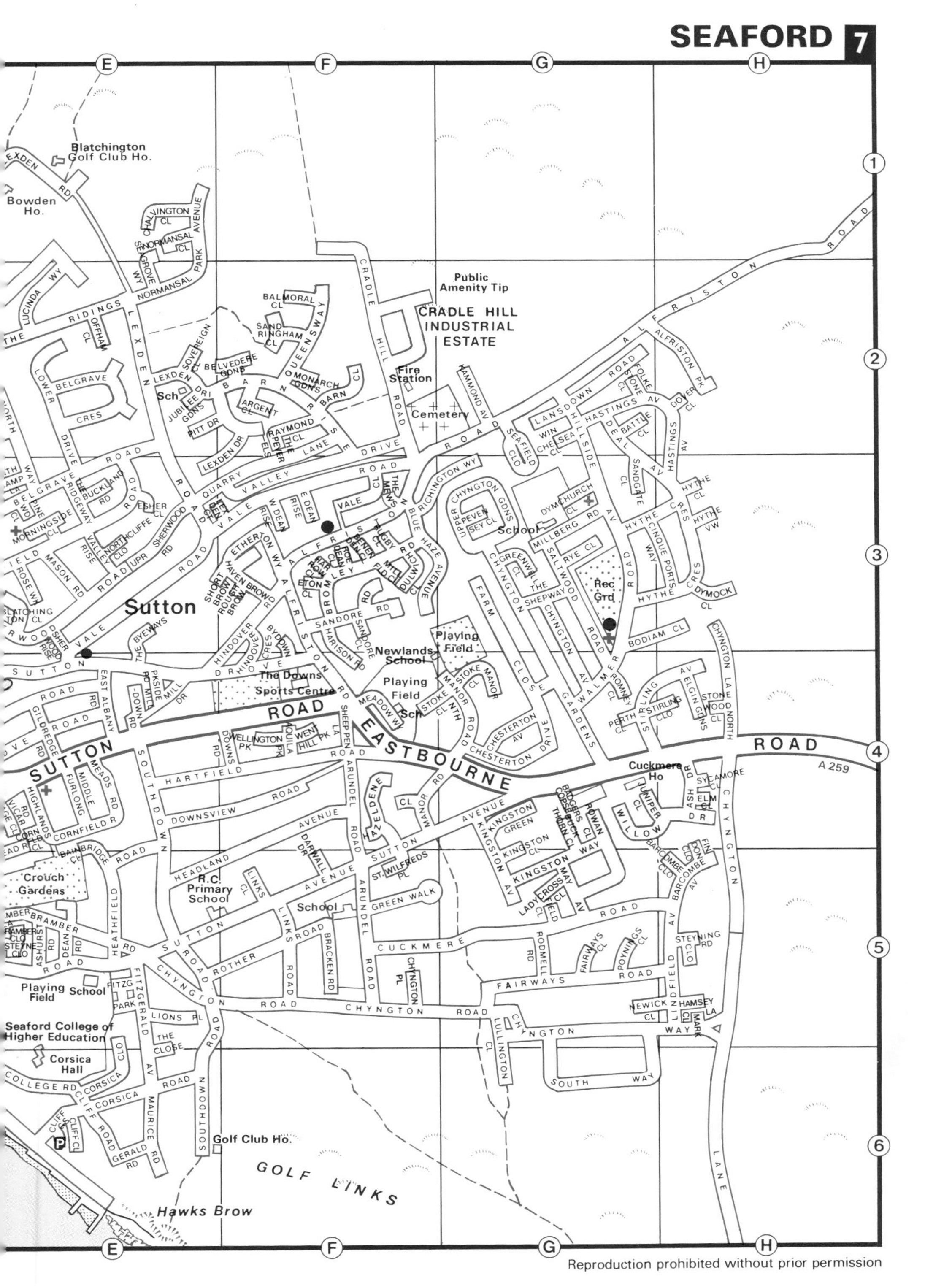
E
F
G
H
1
2
3
4
5
6
Blatchington Golf Club Ho.
Bowden Ho.
Public Amenity Tip
CRADLE HILL INDUSTRIAL ESTATE
Fire Station
Cemetery
Sutton
School
Rec Grd
Playing Field
Newlands School
The Downs Sports Centre
Playing Field
Sch
SUTTON ROAD
EASTBOURNE ROAD
ROAD
A 259
Cuckmere Ho
R.C. Primary School
School
Crouch Gardens
Playing Field
School
Seaford College of Higher Education
Corsica Hall
Golf Club Ho.
GOLF LINKS
Hawks Brow
ALFRISTON ROAD
LEXDEN RD
CHYNGTON ROAD
CHYNGTON LANE
CHYNGTON WAY
SOUTH WAY
CUCKMERE ROAD
SUTTON AVENUE
HEADLAND AVENUE
DOWNSVIEW ROAD
HARTFIELD ROAD
SOUTHDOWN ROAD
QUARRY ROAD
VALLEY ROAD
BARN RISE
QUEENSWAY
CRADLE HILL ROAD
ARUNDEL ROAD
FAIRWAYS ROAD
SUTTON PARK ROAD
CHYNGTON GARDENS
WALMER ROAD
HILLSIDE AV
HASTINGS AV
HYTHE CRES
FARM CLOSE
CHESTERTON DRIVE
KINGSTON WAY
LINDFIELD AV
BARCOMBE AV
CORSICA ROAD
MAURICE RD
CLIFF ROAD
GERALD RD
FITZGERALD AV
COLLEGE RD
BRAMBER ROAD
HEATHFIELD ROAD
NORMANSAL PARK AVENUE
THE RIDINGS
BELGRAVE CRES
LOWER DRIVE
SUTTON DROVE

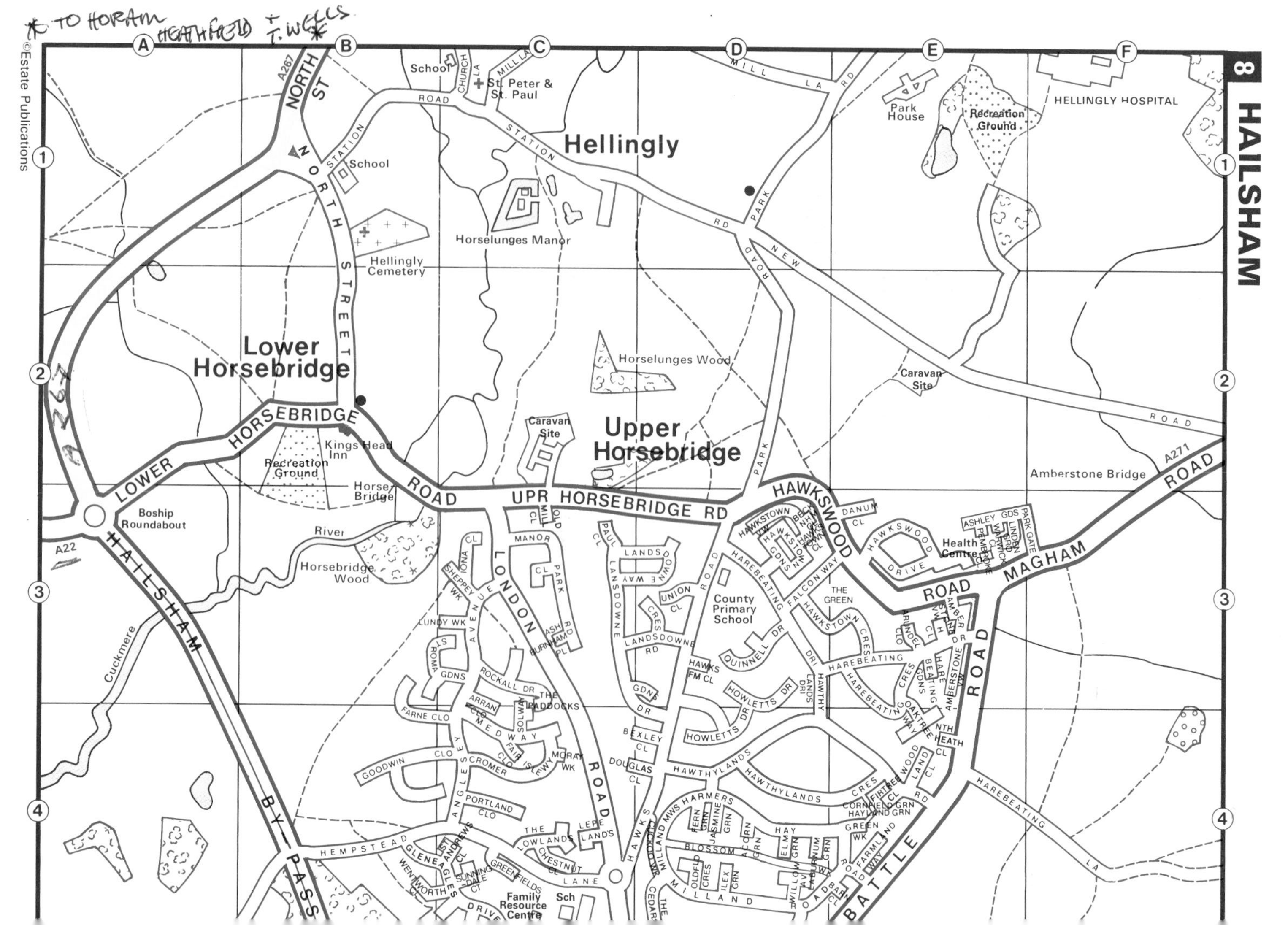

TO HORAM HEATHFIELD + T.WELLS
HELLINGLY HOSPITAL
Recreation Ground
Park House
MILL LA RD
School
CHURCH LA
MILL LA
St. Peter & St. Paul
STATION ROAD
Hellingly
PARK RD
NEW ROAD
Horselunges Manor
Hellingly Cemetery
Horselunges Wood
Caravan Site
NORTH ST
A267
NORTH STREET
STATION
School
Lower Horsebridge
Upper Horsebridge
LOWER HORSEBRIDGE ROAD
Kings Head Inn
Recreation Ground
Horse Bridge
UPR HORSEBRIDGE RD
Amberstone Bridge
A271
ROAD
MAGHAM ROAD
Boship Roundabout
A22
River
Horsebridge Wood
Cuckmere
HAILSHAM BY-PASS
HAWKSWOOD
HAWKSWOOD DRIVE
DANUM CL
ASHLEY GDS
PARK GATE
LINDEN GRO
WARWICK CL
PEMBROKE CL
Health Centre
HAWKSTOWN VW
HAWKSTOWN GDNS
HAWKSTOWN CL
HAWKSTOWN CRES
FALCON WAY
THE GREEN
HAREBEATING ROAD
HAREBEATING DRI
HAREBEATING CRES
HAREBEATING GDNS
HAREBEATING LA
County Primary School
QUINNELL DR
HAWKS FM CL
HOWLETTS DR
HOWLETTS
HAWTHYLANDS DRI
HAWTHYLANDS
HAWTHYLANDS CRES
ARUNDEL CLO
AMBERSTONE VW
OAKTREE WAY
HEATH CL
WOODLAND CL
FIRTREE
CORNFIELD GRN
HAYLAND GRN
GREEN WK
FARMLAND WAY
BATTLE ROAD
MANOR PARK
OLD MILL CL
PAUL CL
LANSDOWNE WAY
LANSDOWNE
LANSDOWNE RD
LANSDOWNE CRES
LANSDOWNE GDNS
LANSDOWNE DR
UNION CL
BEXLEY CL
DOUGLAS CL
ASH RD
BURNHAM PL
LONDON ROAD
IONA CL
SHEPPEY WK
AVENUE
LUNDY WK
ROMA GDNS
ROCKALL DR
THE PADDOCKS
ARRAN CLO
SOLWAY
MEDWAY
FAIR ISLE CLO
MORAY WK
FARNE CLO
GOODWIN CLO
CROMER
ANGLESEY
PORTLAND CLO
HEMPSTEAD LA
GLENEAGLES
ST ANDREWS CL
WENTWORTH
SUNNINGDALE CT
GREENFIELDS
THE LOWLANDS
CHESTNUT CL
LEPELANDS
LANE
Family Resource Centre
Sch
DRIVE
HAWKS
CUCKOO WK
MILLAND MWS
HARMERS
FERN GRN
JASMINE GRN
ACORN GRN
HAY
ELM GRN
LABURNUM
WILLOW GRN
BLOSSOM
OLDFIELD CRES
ILEX GRN
MILLAND
THE CEDARS

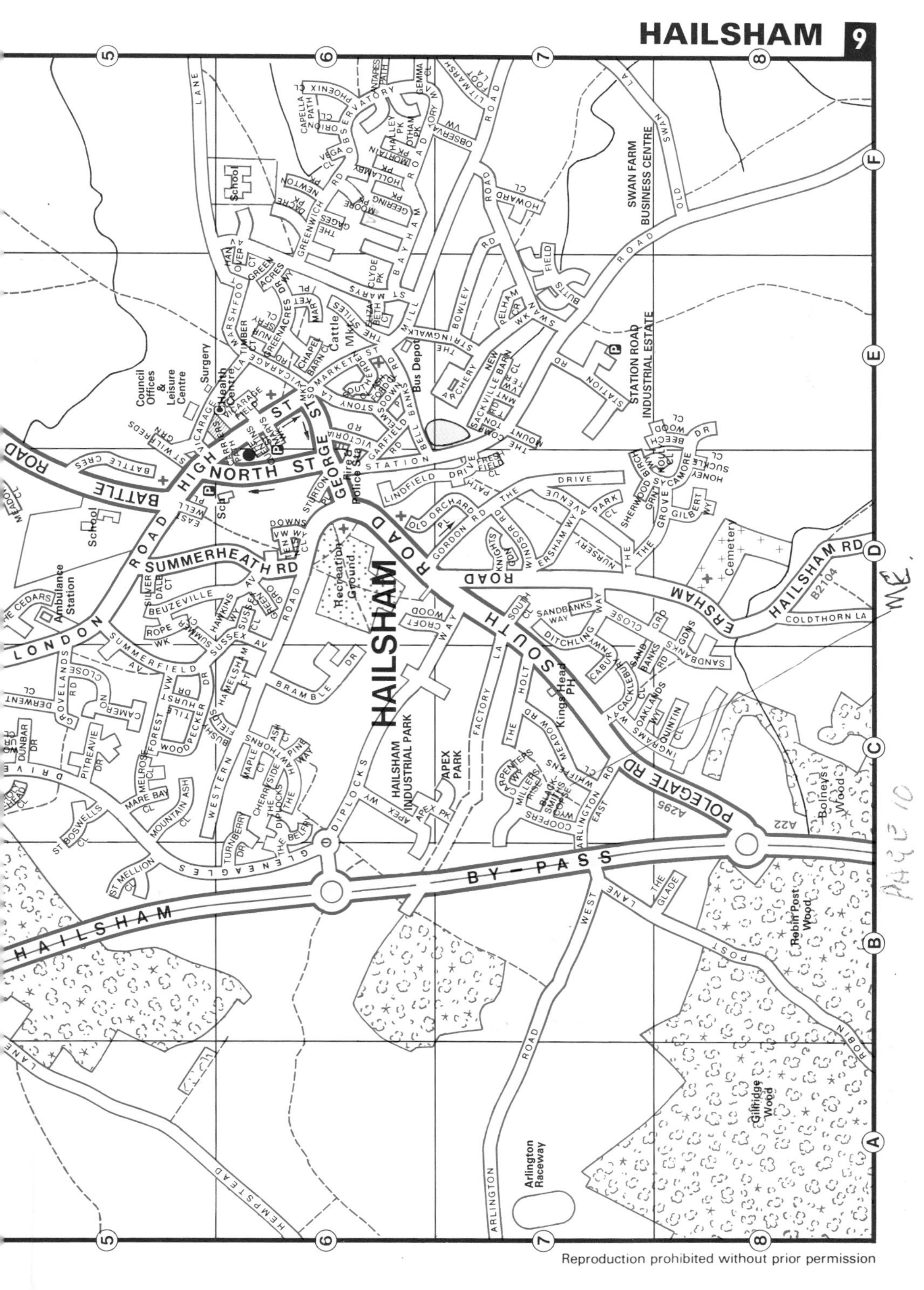
HAILSHAM
HAILSHAM INDUSTRIAL PARK
APEX PARK
SWAN FARM BUSINESS CENTRE
STATION ROAD INDUSTRIAL ESTATE
Recreation Ground
Cemetery
Council Offices & Leisure Centre
Health Centre
Surgery
School
Sch
Ambulance Station
Fire Stn
Police Sta
Bus Depot
Cattle Mkt
Kings Head PH
Arlington Raceway
Gilridge Wood
Robin Post Wood
Boleneys Wood
NORTH ST
HIGH ST
GEORGE ST
MARKET ST
BATTLE ROAD
BATTLE CRES
LONDON ROAD
SUMMERHEATH RD
SOUTH ROAD
POLEGATE RD
ERSHAM ROAD
HAILSHAM RD
B2104
COLDTHORN LA
A295
A22
HAILSHAM BY-PASS
ARLINGTON ROAD WEST
ARLINGTON ROAD EAST
HEMPSTEAD LANE
SWAN ROAD
STATION ROAD
DIPLOCKS WY
APEX WY
APEX PK
BRAMBLE DR
WESTERN RD
FACTORY LA
GLENEAGLES DR
ST MELLION CL
ST BOSWELLS CL
MOUNTAIN ASH CL
MARE BAY CL
MELROSE CL
PITREAVIE DR
DUNBAR DR
DERWENT CL
GROVELANDS RD
GROVELANDS CLOSE
CAMERON
FOREST VW
WOODPECKER
SUMMERFIELD AV
SUSSEX AV
ROPE WK
HAWKINS WY
BEUZEVILLE
SILVER DALE CT
THE CEDARS
OBSERVATORY VW
PHOENIX CL
CAPELLA PATH
ORION CL
VEGA CL
ANTARES PATH
GEMMA CL
HALLEY PK
OTHAM PK
MORTAIN PK
HOLLAMBY PK
NEWTON PK
GEERING PK
MOORE PK
DACRE PK
THE GAGES
GREENWICH RD
BAYHAM ROAD
LITMARSH
HOWARD CL
BOWLEY RD
BUTTS FIELD
ST MARYS WK
CLYDE PK
THE STILES
ELIZABETH CT
MILL RD
STRINGWALK
PELHAM CR
SWAN WK
ARCHERY
NEW BARN CL
SACKVILLE RD
MOUNT PLEASANT
THE COMMON
BELL BANKS RD
STONY LA
VICTORIA RD
GARFIELD RD
STATION RD
LINDFIELD DRIVE
FRESH FIELD CL
OLD ORCHARD RD
GORDON RD
KNIGHTS GDN
WINDSOR RD
ERSHAM WY
NURSERY PATH
THE AVENUE
PARK CL
THE DRIVE
THE GROVE
SHERWOOD GRN
BIRCH WY
HOLLY CL
BEECH WOOD CL
SYCAMORE DR
HONEY SUCKLE CL
GILBERT WY
SANDBANKS WAY
SANDBANKS CLOSE
SANDBANKS GDNS
SANDBANKS GRD
DITCHLING WAY
CABURN
CACKLEBURY CL
OAKLANDS WY
QUINTIN CL
INGRAMS WAY
THE HOLT
MEADOW RD
WHIFFENS CL
CARPENTERS WY
MILLERS RISE
BLACKSMITHS COPSE
COOPERS WY
CROFT WOOD
CROFT WAY
THE GLADE
POST LANE
ROBIN POST LANE
SWAN LA
OLD ROAD
SUMMERHEATH
DOWNS VW
STURTON PL
EASTWELL PL
ST WILFREDS GRN
VICARAGE RD
VICARAGE FIELD
MARSHFOOT LA
TIMBER CT
GREENACRES DR
GREEN ACRES WY
HANOVER CT
CHAPEL BARN
MARKET PL
CHERRYSIDE
MAPLE CT
HAWTHORNS
ASH CT
PINE WAY
THE HAVEN
THE DIPLOCKS
THE BELFRY
TURNBERRY DR
HAMELSHAM CT
BUSHY FIELDS
TILEHURST DR
WARE

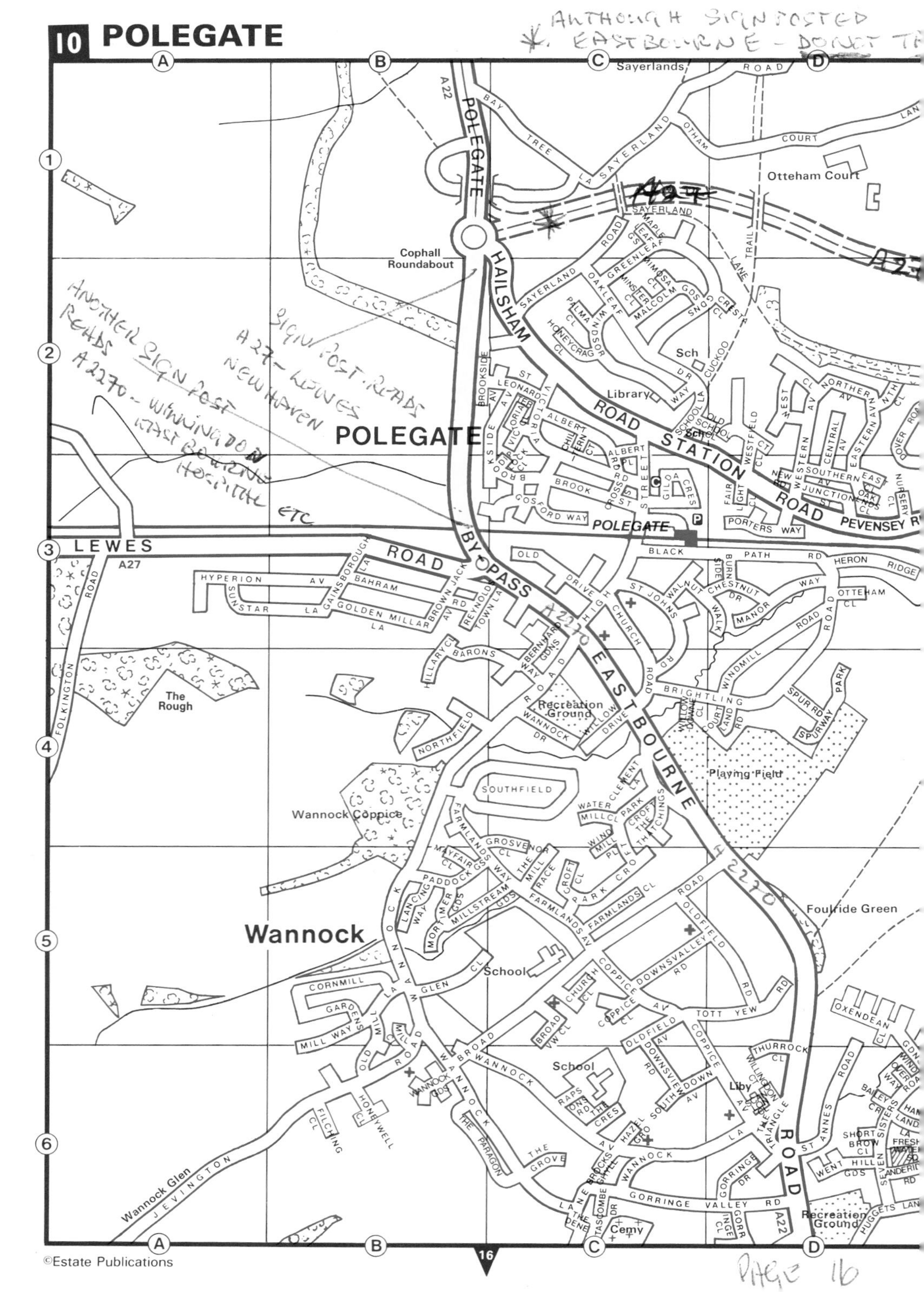
A
B
C
D
1
2
3
4
5
6
Sayerlands
A22
POLEGATE
BAY TREE LA
SAYERLAND ROAD
OTHAM COURT LANE
Otteham Court
A27
SAYERLAND
Cophall Roundabout
HAILSHAM ROAD
SAYERLAND RD
MAPLE LEAF GDNS
GREENLEAF GDNS
MIMOSA CL
MINSTER CL
OAKLEAF CL
MALCOLM GDS
CREST CL
PALMA CL
HONEYCRAG CL
WINDSOR WAY
TRAIL LANE
CUCKOO DR
Sch
Library
BROOKSIDE AV
ST LEONARDS
VICTORIA AV
ALBERT
CHILTERN CL
POLEGATE
STATION ROAD
SCHOOL LA
OLD SCHOOL
WESTFIELD CT
WEST CL
NORTHERN AV
EASTERN AV
DOVER RD
CENTRAL AV
WESTERN AV
SOUTHERN AV
JUNCTION RD
OAKLANDS
NURSERY
NEW RD
FAIR LIGHT CL
PORTERS WAY
PEVENSEY RD
BROOK ST
CROSS ST
STREET
GILDA CRES
GOSFORD WAY
POLEGATE
BLACK PATH RD
HERON RIDGE
LEWES ROAD
A27
FOLKINGTON ROAD
HYPERION AV
SUNSTAR LA
GAINSBOROUGH LA
BAHRAM
GOLDEN MILLAR LA
BROWN JACK AV
REYNOLDS RD
TOWN LA
BY-PASS
OLD DRIVE
HIGH ST
ST JOHNS RD
WALNUT WALK
CHESTNUT DR
MANOR WAY
OTTEHAM CL
WINDMILL ROAD
CHURCH RD
BARONS WAY
HILLARY CL
BERNHARD GDNS
EASTBOURNE
The Rough
ROAD
Recreation Ground
WILLOW DRIVE
WANNOCK DR
BRIGHTLING
WILLOW COURT
DOWNE CL
LAND RD
SPUR RD
PARK
SPURWAY
NORTHFIELD
SOUTHFIELD
Playing Field
Wannock Coppice
CLEMENT LA
WATER MILL CL
PARK CROFT
THE THATCHINGS
FARMLANDS
GROSVENOR CL
MAYFAIR CL
WIND MILL PL
CROFT CL
THE MILL RACE
PADDOCK GDS
WAY
LANCING WAY
MORTIMER GDS
MILLSTREAM GDS
FARMLANDS AV
FARMLANDS CL
ROAD
OLDFIELD RD
Foulride Green
Wannock
School
CORNMILL GARDENS
GLEN CL
WANNOCK
MILL LA
COPPICE
CHURCH CL
DOWNSVALLEY RD
TOTT YEW RD
OXENDEAN
MILL WAY
MILL ROAD
OLD
BROAD ROAD
BROAD VW CL
COPPICE CL
OLDFIELD AV
DOWNSVIEW RD
COPPICE AV
THURROCK CL
School
WANNOCK GDS
WANNOCK
Liby
WILLINGDON AV
SOUTHDOWN AV
RAPSONS RD
THE CRES
HAZEL GRO
THE TRIANGLE
ROAD
ST ANNES RD
FILCHING CL
HONEYWELL CL
THE PARAGON
THE GROVE
WANNOCK LA
BROCKS GHYLL
GORRINGE DR
SHORT BROW
WENT HILL GDS
SEVEN SISTERS
BAILEY CRES
Wannock Glen
JEVINGTON
LANE
TASCOMBE DR
THE DENE
GORRINGE VALLEY RD
GORRINGE CL
A22
Recreation Ground
HUGGETTS LANE
Cemy
16

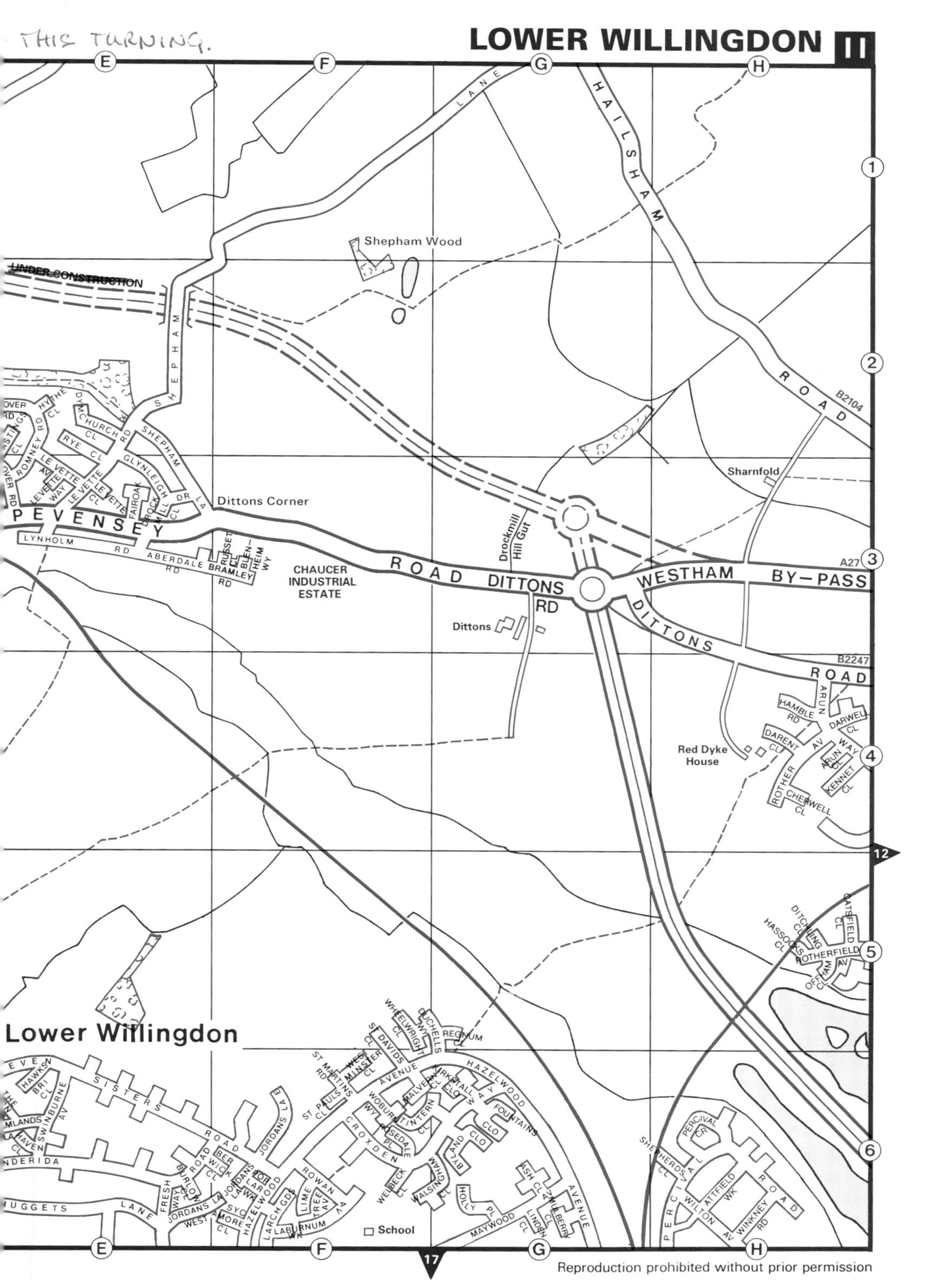

THIS TURNING.

E F G H

1

Shepham Wood

UNDER CONSTRUCTION

2

B2104

Sharnfold

PEVENSEY

Dittons Corner

CHURCH CL
RYE CL
LE VETTE
AV
LE VETTE
WAY
LE VETTE CL
FAIROAK
GLYNLEIGH DR LA
SHEPHAM
SHEPHAM RD
ROMNEY RD
HYTHE
LOVER RD

LYNHOLM RD
ABERDALE RD
BRAMLEY
SUSSEX
RD
BLEN-
HEIM
WY

CHAUCER
INDUSTRIAL
ESTATE

Drockmill
Hill Gut

ROAD DITTONS
RD

Dittons

WESTHAM BY-PASS

A27 3

DITTONS

ROAD

B2247

HAMBLE
RD
ARUN
AV
DARWEL
CL
DARENT
CL
ARUN
WAY
KENNET
CL
ROTHER
CL
CHERWELL
CL

Red Dyke
House

4

12

OATSFIELD
DITCHLING
CL
HASSOCKS
CL
ROTHERFIELD
OFFHAM AV

5

Lower Willingdon

WHEELWRIGHT
MITCHELLS
REGNUM
ST DAVIDS
AV
WEST
MINSTER
MALVERN
MARSHALL AV
HAZELWOOD
FOUNTAINS
ST PAULS CL
ST MARTINS CL
WEBURN
INTERN
ROSEDALE
CLOXDEN
WYLAND
CLO
WELBECK
WINWOOD
WALSINGH
HOLLY
MAYWOOD PL
LINDEN
ASH CL
BERRY
AVENUE

THE
EVEN
HAWKEN
BRI
SISTERS
SWINBURNE
MLANDS
AV
RAVEN
NDERIDA
ROAD
BER
JORDANS LA
BIRCH WOOD
FRESH WAY
JORDANS CL
WEST
MORE CL
HAZELWOOD
SYG
ROWAN
LIME
TREV
AV
LARCH RD
LABURNUM

NUGGETS LANE

SHEPHERDS LA
PERCIVAL
WILTON AV
ATTFIELD WK
WINKNEY RD
PERCIVAL ROAD

6

□ School

E F 17 G H

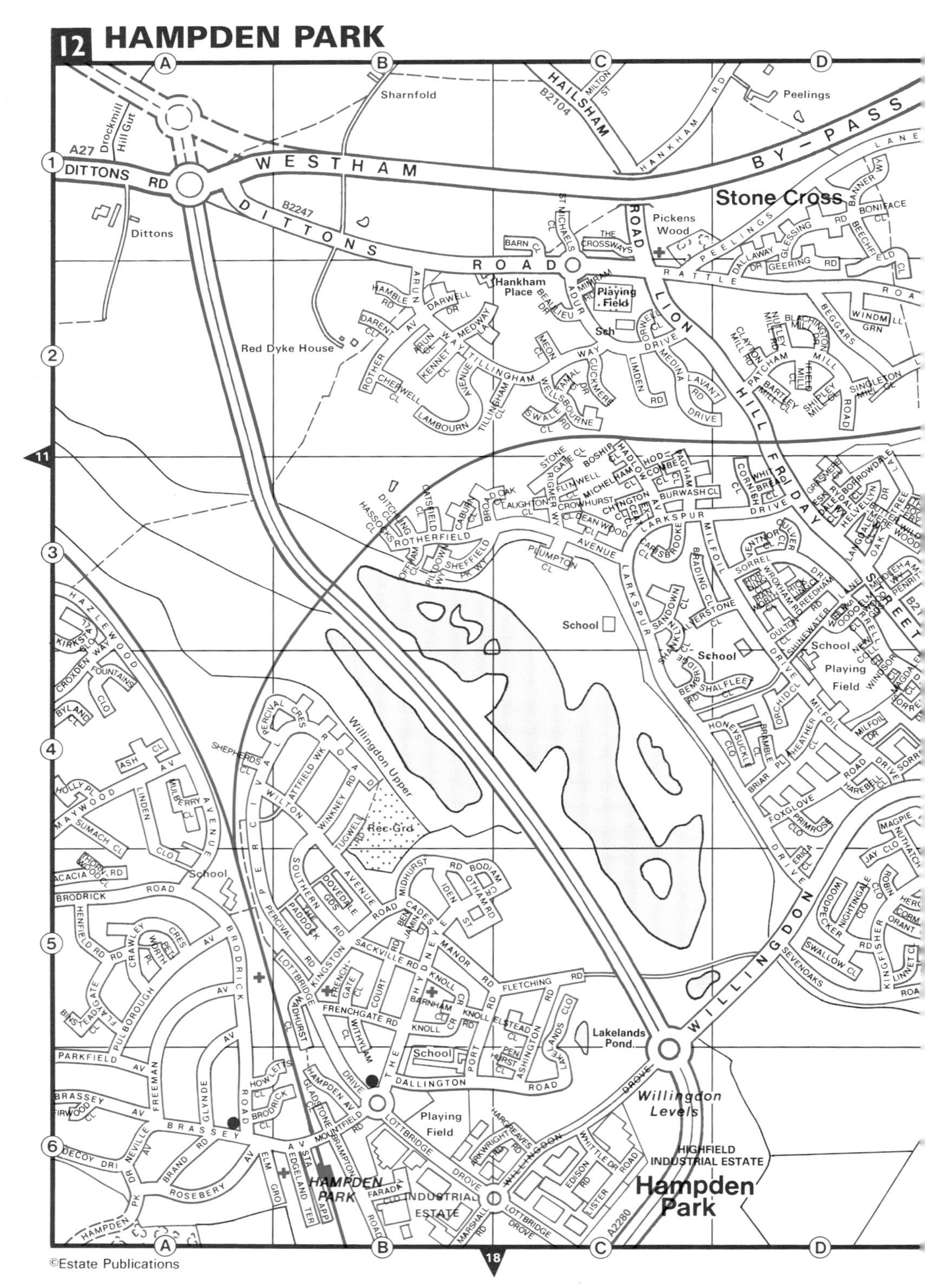

12
HAMPDEN PARK
A
B
C
D
1
2
3
4
5
6
11
18
A27
Drockmill
Hill Gut
DITTONS RD
WESTHAM BY-PASS
B2247
DITTONS ROAD
Dittons
Sharnfold
HAILSHAM RD
B2104
MILTON ST
HANKHAM RD
Peelings
Stone Cross
Pickens Wood
PEELINGS LANE
RATTLE ROAD
BANNER WY
BONIFACE CL
BEECHFIELD CL
GLESSING RD
GEERING RD
DALLAWAY DR
WINDMILL GRN
BEGGARS
BLACKINGTON MILL DR
NUTLEY MILL RD
CLAYTON MILL RD
PATCHAM MILL CL
BARTLEY MILL CL
SHIPLEY MILL CL
SINGLETON MILL CL
ROAD
LION HILL
FRIDAY STREET
ST MICHAELS CL
THE CROSSWAYS
BARN CL
Hankham Place
Playing Field
Sch
ADUR DR
BEAULIEU DR
ORWELL CL
DRIVE
MEDINA
LAVANT RD
DRIVE
LIMDEN RD
CUCKMERE
TAMAR
WELLSBOURNE
SWALE CL
MEON CL
WAY
TILLINGHAM
TILLINGHAM CL
AVENUE
KENNET CL
ARUN CL
WAY
MEDWAY LA
DARWELL DR
ARUN
HAMBLE RD
DARENT CL
AV
ROTHER
CHERWELL CL
LAMBOURN
Red Dyke House
STONE GATE CL
BOSHIP CL
HADLOW CL
HODCOMBE CL
PAGHAM CL
FLIMWELL
MICHELHAM CL
RIGMER WY
CROWHURST
CHYNGTON
BURWASH CL
LARKSPUR
LARKSPUR DRIVE
DEAN WOOD CL
AVENUE
LAUGHTON CL
BROAD OAK CL
CABURN
CATSFIELD CL
DITCHLING
HASSOCKS CL
ROTHERFIELD
SHEFFIELD PK WY
PILTDOWN WY
OFFHAM
PLUMPTON CL
CARISBROOKE
BRADING CL
MILFOIL
VENTNOR
CULVER
SORREL
WROXHAM RD
SANDOWN CL
TOTLAND
ALVERSTONE CL
SHANKLIN CL
BEMBRIDGE RD
SHALFLEET CL
School
School
School
Playing Field
CORNISH CL
WHITEBREAD CL
HONEYSUCKLE CLO
BRAMBLE CL
BRIAR PL
HEATHER CL
ORCHID CL
MILFOIL DR
HAREBELL CL
FOXGLOVE
PRIMROSE
CLO
ERICA CL
DRIVE
OULTON CL
SHINEWATER LANE
MAGPIE
NUTHATCH
JAY CLO
ROBIN CLO
NIGHTINGALE CLO
WOODPECKER
KINGFISHER
SWALLOW CL
LINNET CL
CORMORANT
HERON
WILLINGDON DROVE
SEVENOAKS
Willingdon Upper
Rec Grd
HAZLEWOOD
KIRKSTALL CLO
CROXDEN WAY
FOUNTAINS CLO
BYLAND CL
ASH CL
AV
HOLLY PL
MAYWOOD
SUMACH CL
MULBERRY CL
LINDEN CLO
AVENUE
ACACIA RD
THORNWOOD CL
School
BRODRICK ROAD
HENFIELD RD
CRAWLEY CRES
WORTH PL
PETWORTH
AV
BRODRICK
FLAXGATE CL
BINSTEAD
PULBOROUGH AV
PARKFIELD AV
FREEMAN AV
GLYNDE AV
BRASSEY AV
FIRWOOD CL
BRASSEY AV
DECOY DRI
NEVILLE AV
BRAND RD
ROSEBERY AV
PK DR
HAMPDEN
HOWLETTS CL
BRODRICK CL
ROAD
PERCIVAL CRES
SHEPHERDS CL
PERCIVAL
WILTON
ATTFIELD WK
WINKNEY RD
TUGWELL RD
ROAD
PERCIVAL
SOUTHERN
THE PADDOCK
DOVEDALE GDS
AVENUE
ROAD
MIDHURST RD
BODIAM CR
OTHAM RD
IDEN ST
CADES
BENJAMIN CL
MANOR
SACKVILLE RD
KINGSTON
LOTTBRIDGE
FRENCHGATE CL
COURT
BARNHAM
KNOLL CR
FLETCHING RD
WADHURST CL
FRENCHGATE RD
KNOLL
WITHYLAM
ELSTEAD
ASHINGTON
LAKELANDS CLO
PENHURST CL
School
DALLINGTON ROAD
Lakelands Pond
HAMPDEN AV
GLADSTONE CL
MOUNTFIELD RD
BRAMPTON
DRIVE
Playing Field
HARGREAVES RD
ARKWRIGHT RD
LOTTBRIDGE DROVE
WILLINGDON DROVE
WHITTLE DR
EDISON RD
LISTER
ROAD
Willingdon Levels
HIGHFIELD INDUSTRIAL ESTATE
Hampden Park
A2280
ELM GRO
EDGELAND TER
STA APP
HAMPDEN PARK
FARADAY CLO
INDUSTRIAL ESTATE
MARSHALL RD
LOTTBRIDGE DROVE
©Estate Publications

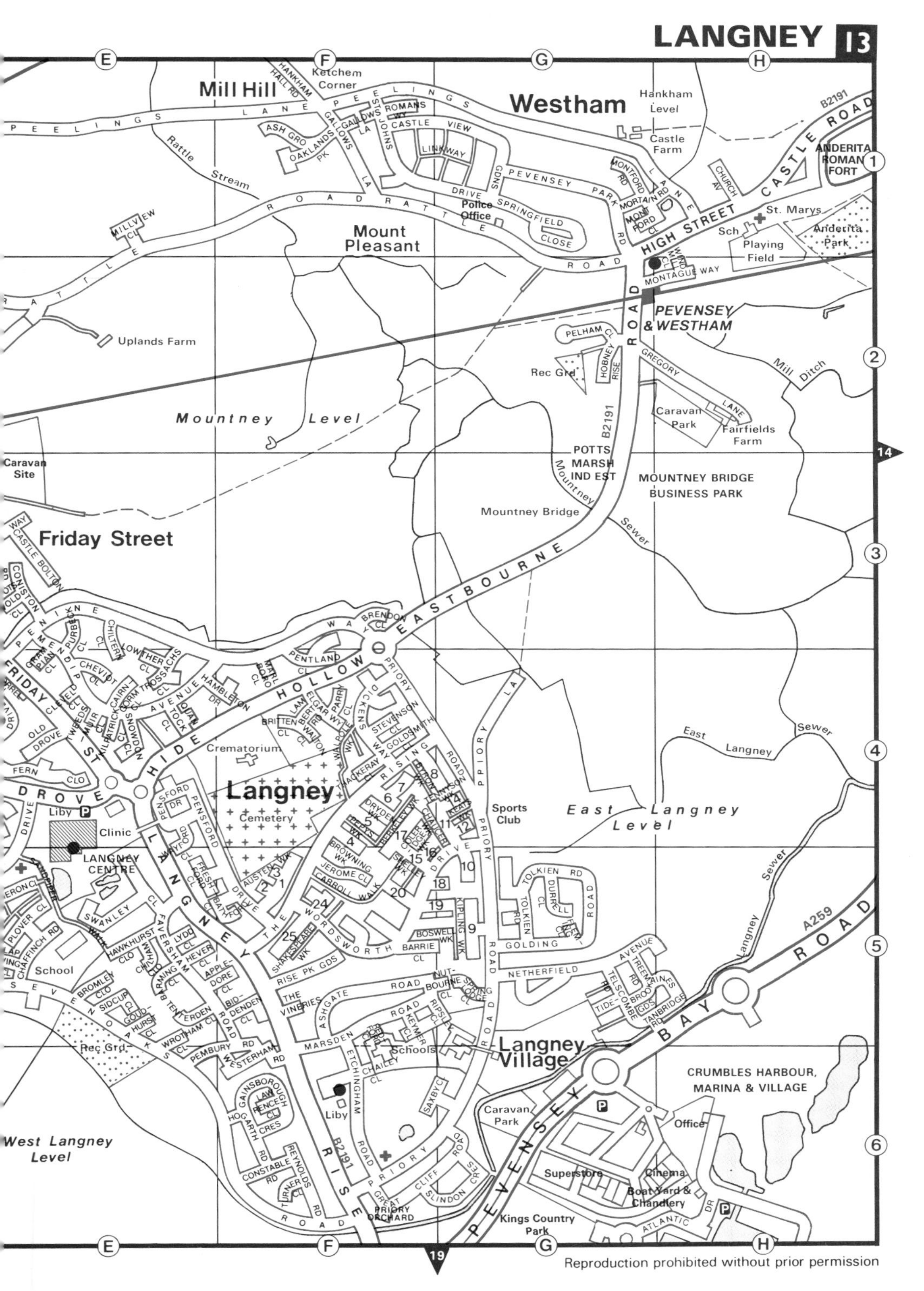

LANGNEY
13
Mill Hill
Ketchem Corner
Westham
Hankham Level
Castle Farm
ANDERITA ROMAN FORT
St. Marys
Sch
Playing Field
Anderita Park
HIGH STREET
CASTLE ROAD
B2191
PEELINGS LANE
Rattle Stream
RATTLE ROAD
MILLVIEW CL
ASH GRO
OAKLANDS PK
GALLOWS LA
ST JOHNS
ROMANS WY
CASTLE VIEW
LINKWAY
PEVENSEY PARK
SPRINGFIELD CLOSE
Police Office
Mount Pleasant
MONTAGUE WAY
PEVENSEY & WESTHAM
Uplands Farm
PELHAM CL
HOBNEY RISE
GREGORY LANE
Rec Grd
Mill Ditch
Caravan Park
Fairfields Farm
Mountney Level
Caravan Site
POTTS MARSH IND EST
MOUNTNEY BRIDGE BUSINESS PARK
Mountney Bridge
Mountney Sewer
Friday Street
EASTBOURNE ROAD
HIDE HOLLOW
BRENDON CL
PENTLAND
PRIORY LA
Crematorium
Langney
Cemetery
East Langney
Sewer
Sports Club
East Langney Level
DROVE RD
Liby
Clinic
LANGNEY CENTRE
LANGNEY RISE
School
Rec Grd
West Langney Level
WORDSWORTH
GOLDING RD
NETHERFIELD AVENUE
A259
PEVENSEY BAY ROAD
Langney Sewer
Langney Village
Schools
Caravan Park
CRUMBLES HARBOUR, MARINA & VILLAGE
Office
Superstore
Cinema
Boat Yard & Chandlery
Kings Country Park
ATLANTIC DR
PRIORY ROAD
GREAT CLIFF
SLINDON CRES
PRIORY ORCHARD
14
19
Reproduction prohibited without prior permission

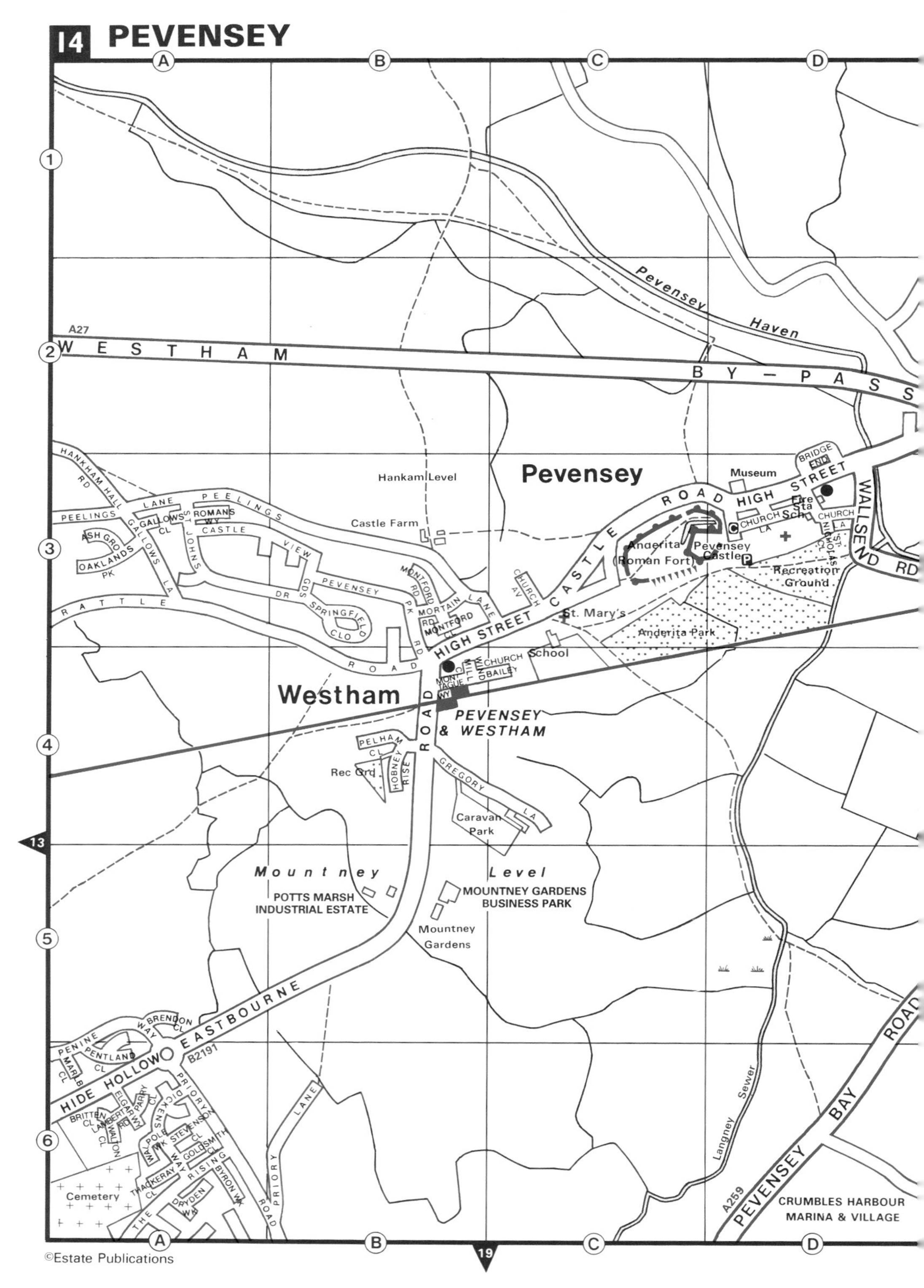

A B C D

1

Pevensey Haven

A27
WESTHAM — BY - PASS

2

Pevensey

Hankam Level

Castle Farm

Museum
BRIDGE END
HIGH STREET
WALLSEND RD

HANHAM HALL RD
PEELINGS LANE
PEELINGS
GALLOWS CL
ROMANS WY
CASTLE
ASH GRO
OAKLANDS PK
GALLOWS LA
ST JOHNS CL
CASTLE VIEW
PEVENSEY DR
SPRINGFIELD CLO
MONTFORD RD
PK
MORTAIN RD
MONTFORD
CHURCH LANE
CHURCH AV
CASTLE ROAD
HIGH STREET

Anderita (Roman Fort)
Pevensey Castle
CHURCH
ST NICHOLAS
Fire Sta
Pre Sch

Recreation Ground

3

RATTLE

St. Mary's

Anderita Park

School

Westham
MONTAGUE CLO
OBAILS
CHURCH

PEVENSEY & WESTHAM

4

ROAD
PELHAM CL
HOBNEY RISE
GREGORY LA
Rec Grd

Caravan Park

13

Mountney   Level

POTTS MARSH INDUSTRIAL ESTATE

MOUNTNEY GARDENS BUSINESS PARK

Mountney Gardens

5

EASTBOURNE
B2191

BRENDON CL
W WAY
PENINE CL
MARB CL
PENTLANS CL
HIDE HOLLOW
PRIORY
EIGHTH AV
DICKENS
POL STEVENSON
GOLDSMITH
RISING
BYRON
PRIORY ROAD
PRIORY LANE

Langney Sewer

PEVENSEY BAY ROAD

6

BRITTEN CL
CLANGET
LANGERT
WAY
POPE
WAL
THACKERAY CL
THE
GARDEN
WAY
RISING

Cemetery

A259
CRUMBLES HARBOUR MARINA & VILLAGE

A B 19 C D

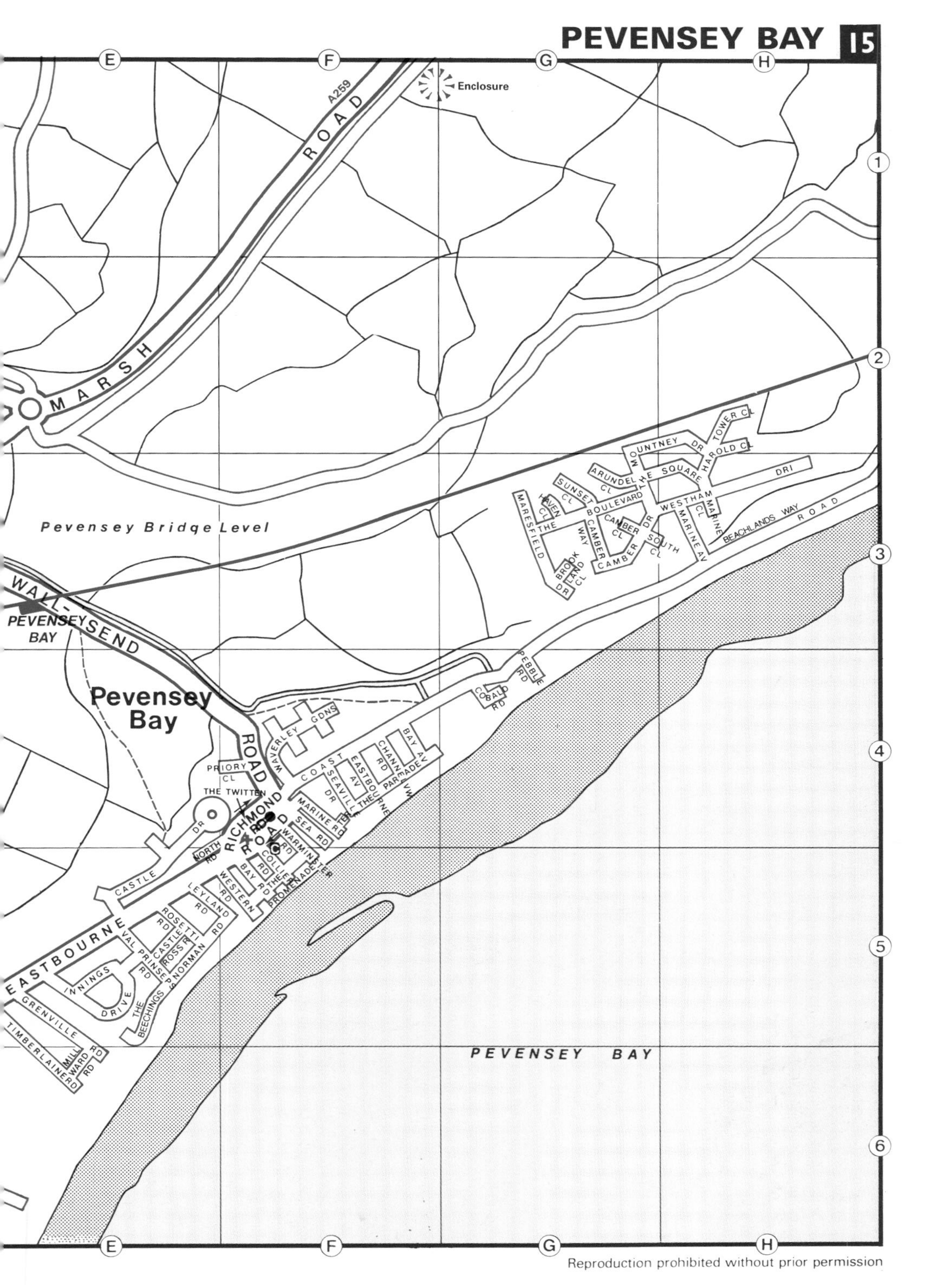

Enclosure

A259

E F G H

R O A D

M A R S H

1

2

Pevensey Bridge Level

3

WALL

PEVENSEY-S END
BAY

**Pevensey
Bay**

PRIORY
CL

THE TWITTEN

RICHMOND ROAD

NORTH
RD

DR

CASTLE

WAVERLEY GDNS

COAST RD

PRIORY RD

WESTERN RD

BAY RD

LEYLAND RD

ROSETTI RD

CASTLE RD

ROSS RD

VAL PRINSEP RD

THE BEECHINGS

NORMAN RD

INNINGS DRIVE

GRENVILLE RD

TIMBERLAINE RD

MILL WARD RD

E A S T B O U R N E

EASTBOURNE RD

MARINE RD

WARMINGS

COLLINGTON RD

THE PROMENADE

SEA RD

SEAVILLE DR

CHANNEL RD

BAY AV

EAST RD

THE PARADE

BAY VW

THE WINELANDS

COTTS
BALD RD

PEBBLE RD

MOUNTNEY DR

TOWER CL

HAROLD CL

ARUNDEL CL

THE SQUARE

MARINE RD

DRI

SUNSET CL

BOULEVARD

WESTHAM CL

HAVEN
THE

MARESFIELD

CAMBER CL

CAMBER DR

MARINE AV

SOUTH

BEACHLANDS WAY

BROOK
DR

ISLAND
CL

CAMBER CL

R O A D

4

5

6

PEVENSEY   BAY

E F G H

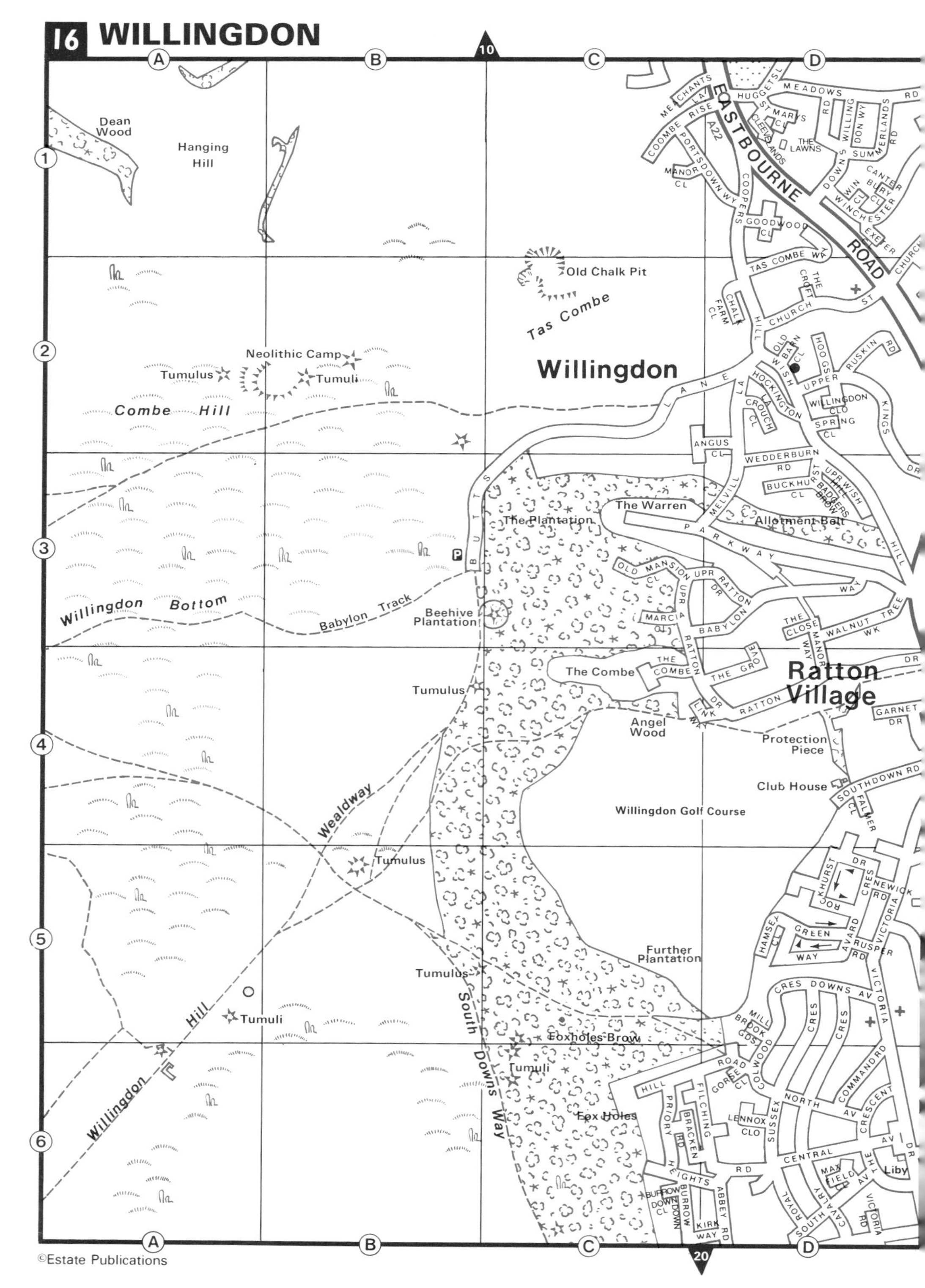

A   B   **10**   C   D

Dean Wood

Hanging Hill

Old Chalk Pit

Tas Combe

Willingdon

EASTBOURNE ROAD

MERCHANTS
COMBE RISE
THE LAWNS
MEADOWS
WILLINGDON WY
PORTSDOWN WY
MANOR CL
GOODWOOD
COOPERS
COMBE WK
CHALK FARM CL
CHURCH ST
THE CROFT
HOGGS LA
RUSKIN CL
OLD BARN
UPPER
HOCKINGTON
CROUCH
WILLINGDON CLO
SPRING CL
KINGS DR

Tumulus
Neolithic Camp
Tumuli

Combe Hill

ANGUS CL

WEDDERBURN RD
UPPWSH
BUCKHURST
BADGERS BANK
MELVILL
HILL

The Plantation

The Warren
Allotment Belt

PARKWAY

BUTTS

Willingdon Bottom

Babylon Track

Beehive Plantation

P

OLD MANSION CL
UPR RATTON DR
MARCH CL
UPR
BABYLON
THE CLOSE
WALNUT TREE WK
WAY

Tumulus

The Combe
THE COMBE

THE GRO
RATTON WAY

Ratton Village

GARNET DR

Wealdway

Angel Wood

Protection Piece

LINK

Tumulus

Willingdon Golf Course

Club House
SOUTHDOWN RD
FALMER

NEWICK
HAMSEY
RDS
CRES
AVARD RD
VICTORIA
RUSPER
GREEN WAY

Willingdon Hill

Tumuli

Further Plantation

CRES DOWNS AV
MILL
BROOK GDNS
CRES
CRES
VICTORIA

South Downs Way

Tumulus

Foxholes Brow
Tumuli

Fox Holes

ROAD
GOREE CLO
FILCHING
PRIORY RD
HILL
BRACKEN CLO
LENNOX CLO
SUSSEX
CENTRAL RD
MAYFIELD
NORTH
THE CRESCENT
COMMAND RD
AV
DOWN CL
ABBEY RD
KIRK
ROYAL
CAVALRY
VICTORIA RD
SOUTH
HEIGHTS
BURROW
BURROW DOWN
Lib

A   B   **20**   C   D

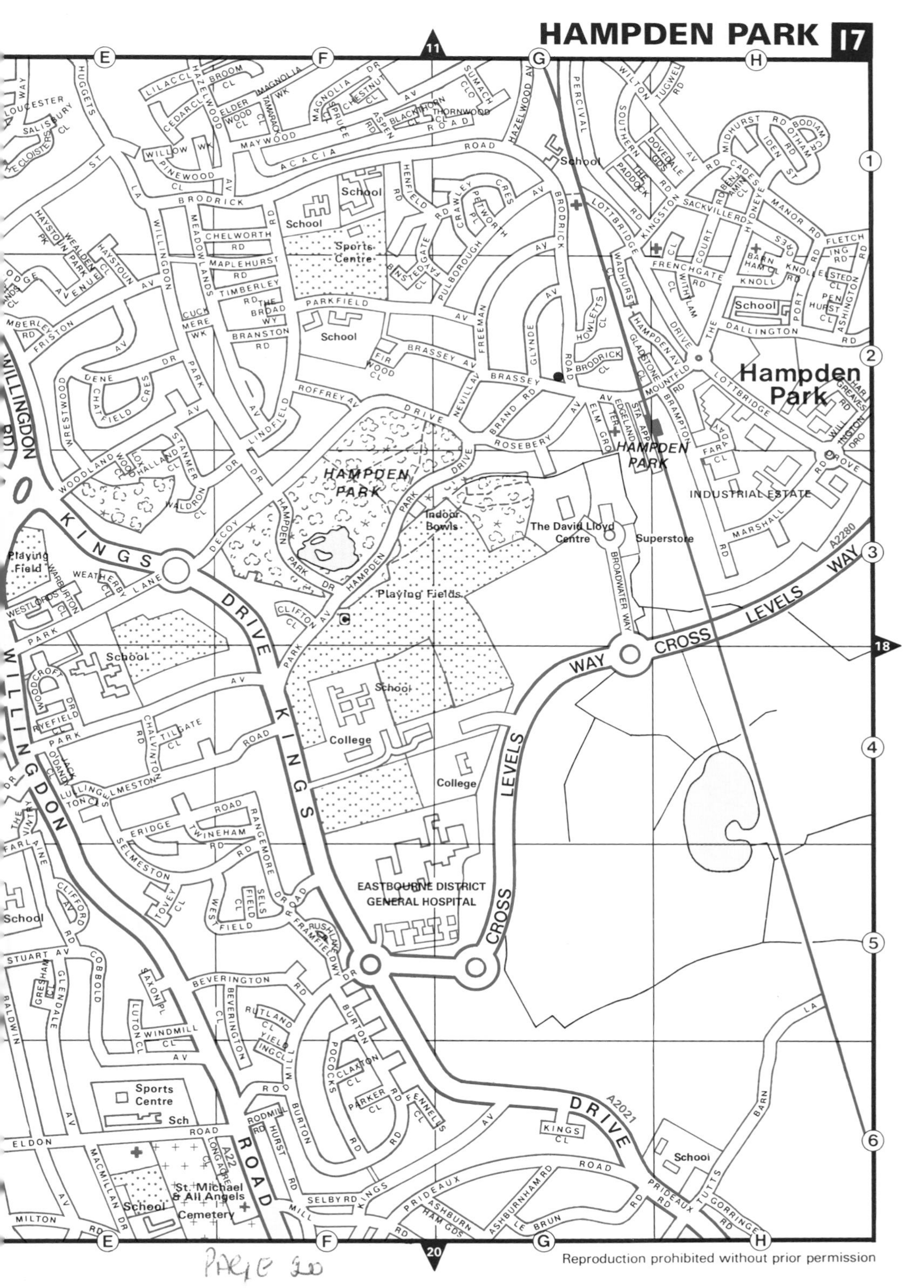

Hampden Park
HAMPDEN PARK
INDUSTRIAL ESTATE
KINGS DRIVE
CROSS LEVELS WAY
A2280
A2021
A22
WILLINGDON ROAD
WILLINGDON RD
DECOY DRIVE
ACACIA ROAD
MAYWOOD AV
BRODRICK RD
BRODRICK ROAD
LOTTBRIDGE DROVE
PARKFIELD AV
BRASSEY AV
ROSEBERY AV
ROFFREY AV
HAMPDEN PARK DRIVE
HAMPDEN AV
BROADWATER WAY
MARSHALL RD
DALLINGTON RD
PRIDEAUX ROAD
ELDON ROAD
MILTON RD
BEVERINGTON ROAD
SELMESTON RD
ERIDGE ROAD
RANGEMORE DR
FRAMFIELD WAY
BURTON RD
WINDMILL AV
STUART AV
BARN LA
School
Sports Centre
Playing Fields
Playing Field
Indoor Bowls
The David Lloyd Centre
Superstore
College
EASTBOURNE DISTRICT GENERAL HOSPITAL
St. Michael & All Angels Cemetery
E
F
G
H
1
2
3
4
5
6
11
18
20

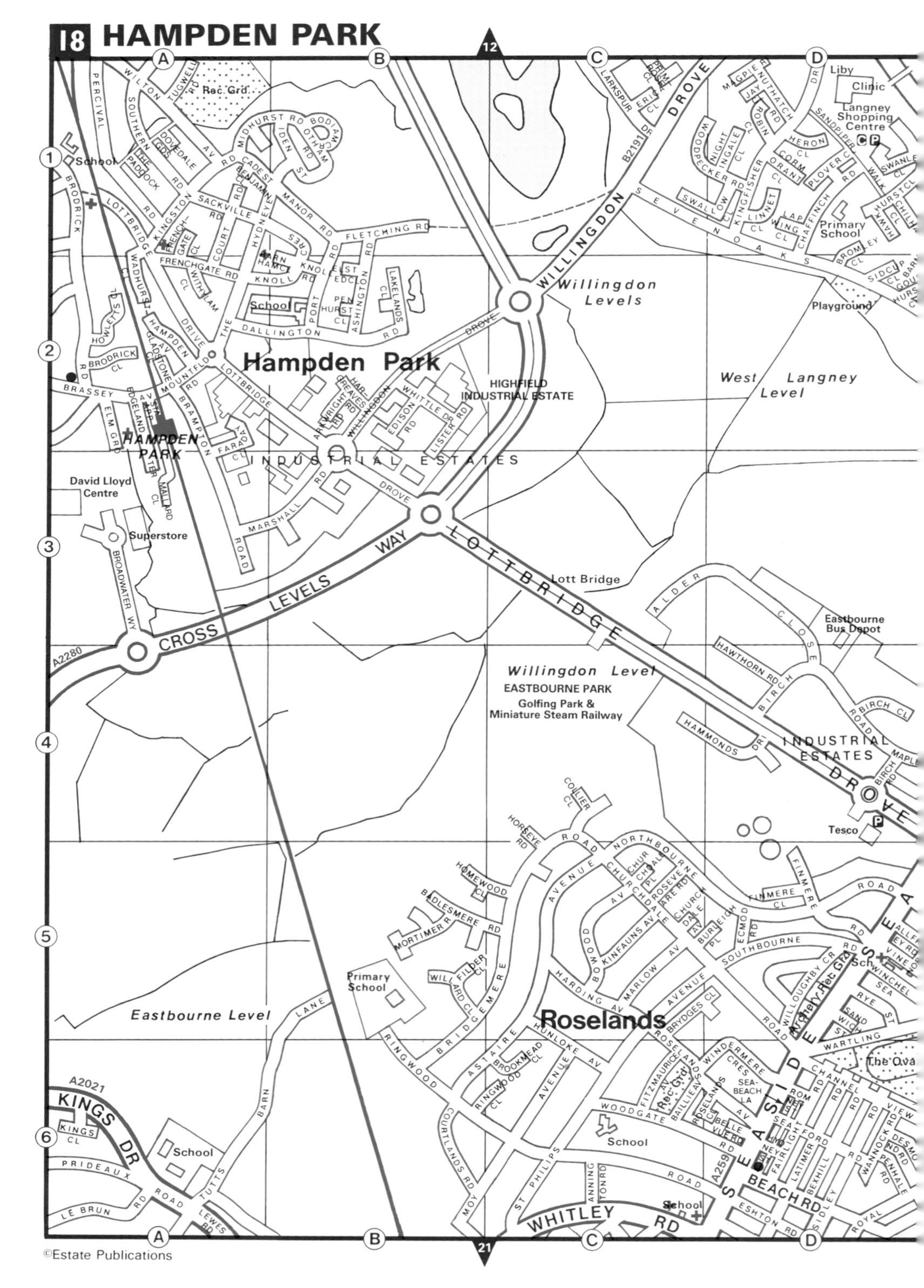

Hampden Park
HAMPDEN PARK
Roselands
Willingdon Levels
West Langney Level
Willingdon Level
Eastbourne Level
HIGHFIELD INDUSTRIAL ESTATE
INDUSTRIAL ESTATES
EASTBOURNE PARK
Golfing Park & Miniature Steam Railway
Lott Bridge
Eastbourne Bus Depot
David Lloyd Centre
Superstore
Langney Shopping Centre
Clinic
Liby
Primary School
Playground
Tesco
Rec. Grd.
School
CROSS LEVELS WAY
LOTTBRIDGE DROVE
WILLINGDON DROVE
KINGS DR
WHITLEY RD
SEASIDE
A2280
A2021
A259
B2191
12
21

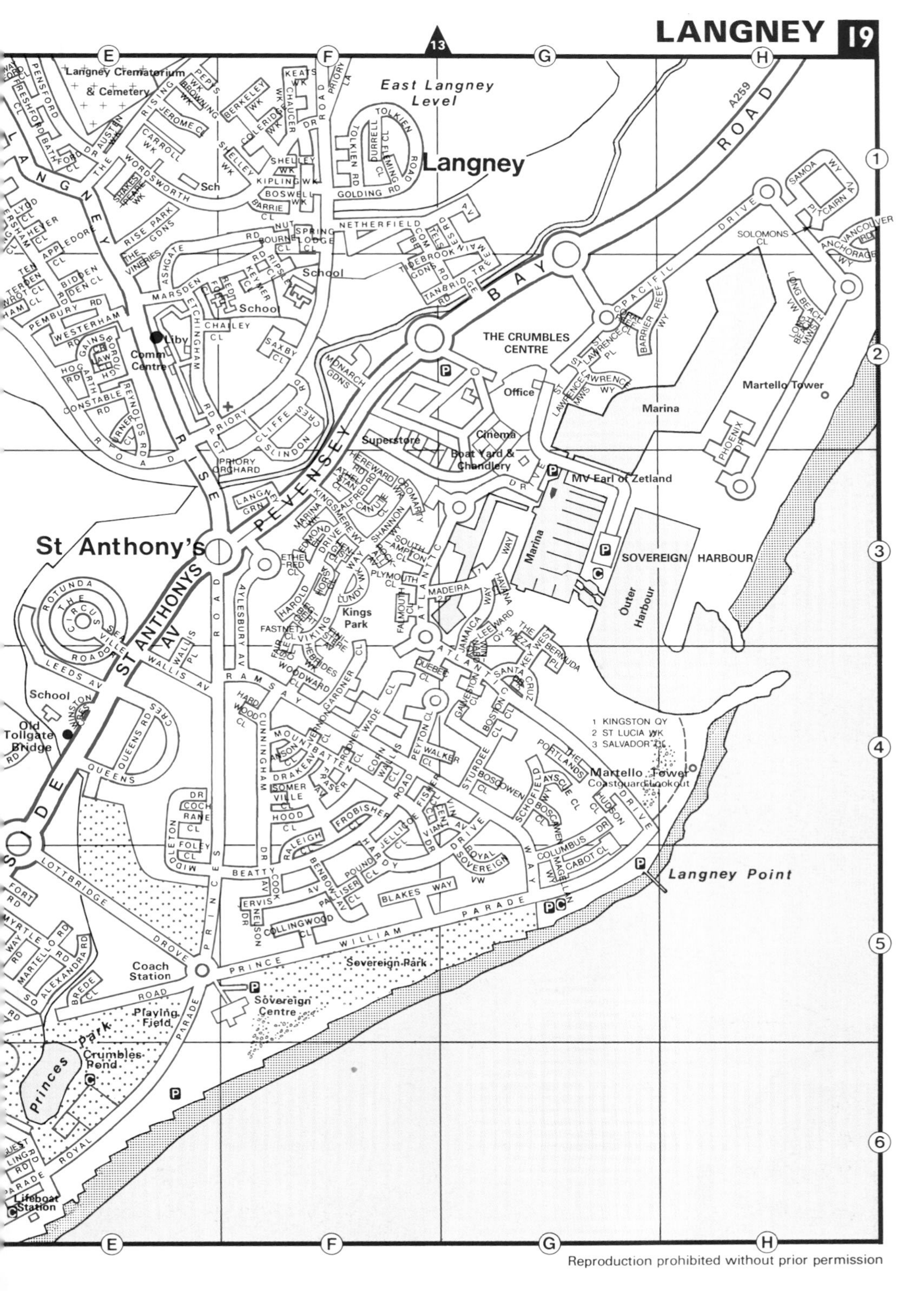
13
East Langney Level
Langney
Langney Crematorium & Cemetery
St Anthony's
THE CRUMBLES CENTRE
SOVEREIGN HARBOUR
Outer Harbour
Marina
Martello Tower
Office
Superstore
Cinema
Boat Yard & Chandlery
MV Earl of Zetland
Kings Park
School
Liby
Comm Centre
Sch
Old Tollgate Bridge
Coach Station
Sovereign Centre
Sovereign Park
Playing Field
Princes Park
Crumbles Pond
Lifeboat Station
Langney Point
Martello Tower
Coastguard Lookout
1 KINGSTON QY
2 ST LUCIA WK
3 SALVADOR CL
A259
BAY ROAD
PEVENSEY
ST ANTHONYS AV
RISE
PRINCE WILLIAM PARADE
PACIFIC DRIVE
ATLANTIC DRIVE
PRINCES ROAD
ROYAL PARADE
LOTTBRIDGE DROVE
PRIORY ROAD
E
F
G
H
1
2
3
4
5
6

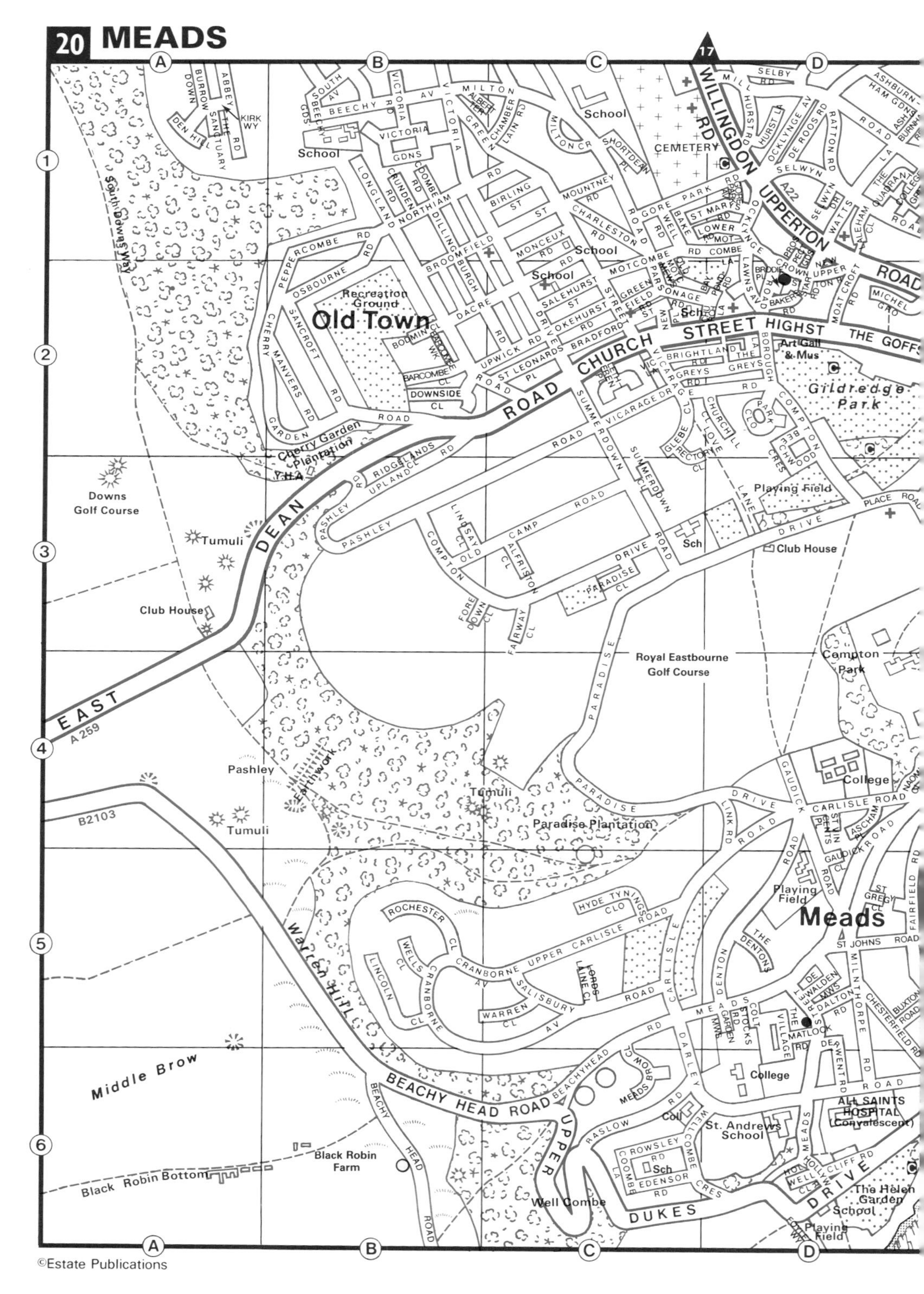
Old Town
Meads
Recreation Ground
Downs Golf Course
Royal Eastbourne Golf Course
Gildredge Park
Compton Park
Paradise Plantation
Cherry Garden Plantation
Middle Brow
Black Robin Bottom
Black Robin Farm
Well Combe
Pashley
Tumuli
Earthwork
South Downs Way
Club House
Cemetery
School
College
St. Andrews School
ALL SAINTS HOSPITAL (Convalescent)
The Helen Garden School
Art Gall & Mus
Playing Field
Y.H.A.
EAST DEAN ROAD
A 259
B2103
CHURCH STREET
HIGH ST
THE GOFFS
WILLINGDON RD
UPPERTON ROAD
A22
BEACHY HEAD ROAD
Warren Hill
DUKES DRIVE
PARADISE DRIVE
CARLISLE ROAD
MEADS RD
COMPTON PLACE ROAD
SUMMERDOWN ROAD
OLD CAMP ROAD
VICARAGE ROAD
UPPER CARLISLE ROAD
SALISBURY ROAD
CRANBORNE AV
WARREN CL
ROCHESTER CL
HYDE TYNINGS CLO
ST JOHNS ROAD
MILNTHORPE RD
DARLEY RD
RASLOW
ROWSLEY RD
EDENSOR
WELLCOMBE CRES
HOLYWELL CLIFF RD
BUXTON ROAD
CHESTERFIELD RD
MATLOCK RD
DERWENT RD
MEADS ST
THE DENTONS
GAUDICK ROAD
LINK RD

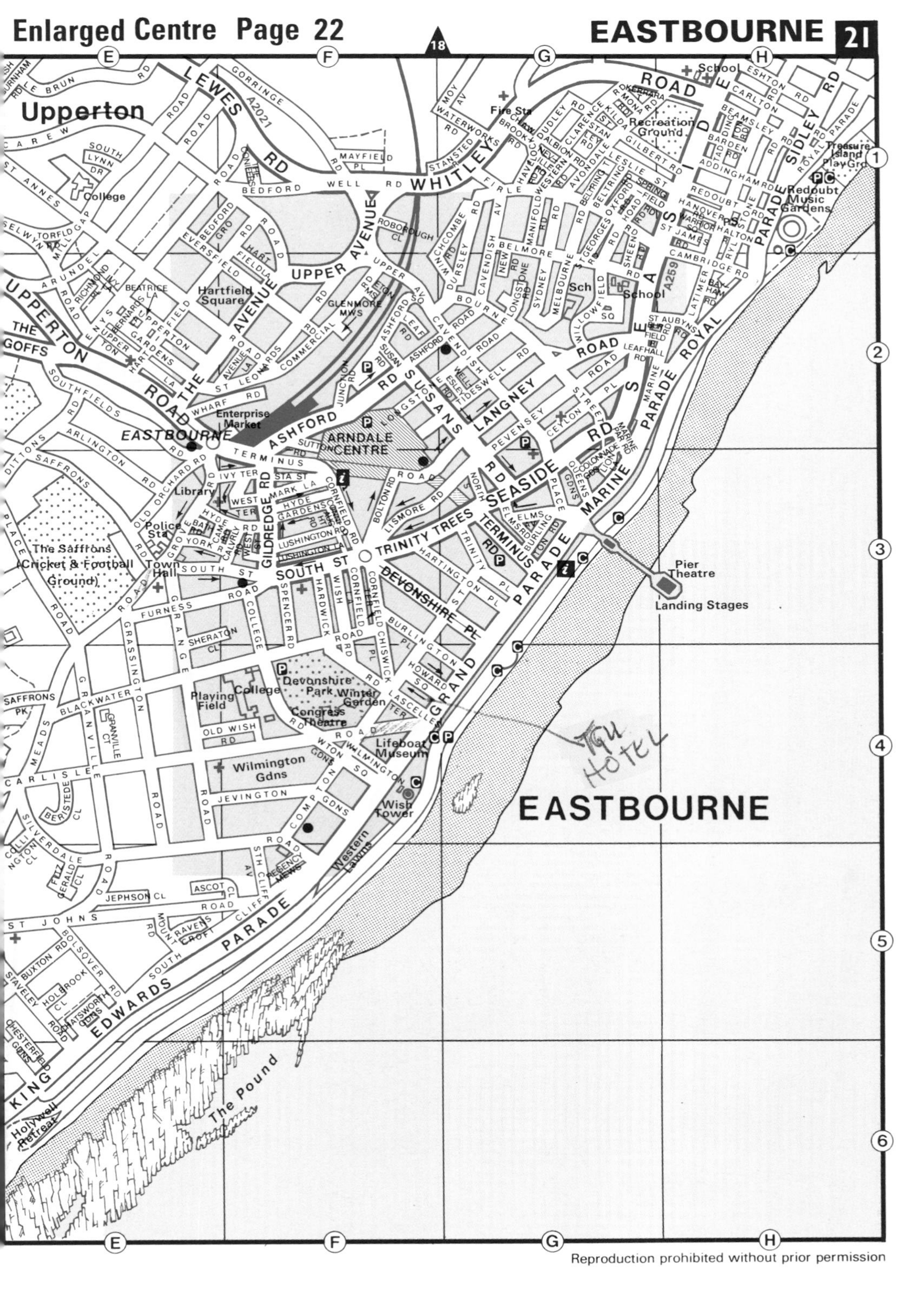
18
E
F
G
H
Upperton
College
Hartfield Square
Enterprise Market
EASTBOURNE
ARNDALE CENTRE
Library
Police Sta
Town Hall
The Saffrons (Cricket & Football Ground)
Fire Sta
Recreation Ground
School
Sch
Treasure Island Play Grd
Redoubt Music Gardens
Pier Theatre
Landing Stages
Devonshire Park
Winter Garden
Congress Theatre
Playing Field
Wilmington Gdns
Lifeboat Museum
Wish Tower
Western Lawns
Holywell Retreat
The Pound
LEWES RD
UPPER AVENUE
WHITLEY RD
BEDFORD WELL RD
UPPERTON RD
THE AVENUE
ASHFORD RD
TERMINUS RD
SOUTH ST
TRINITY TREES
SEASIDE RD
LANGNEY RD
SUSANS RD
CAVENDISH PL
ROYAL PARADE
MARINE PARADE
GRAND PARADE
DEVONSHIRE PL
SEASIDE
KING EDWARDS PARADE
GILDREDGE RD
CORNFIELD RD
CARLISLE RD
MEADS RD
SAFFRONS RD
ST JOHNS RD
SOUTHFIELDS RD
ARLINGTON RD
GRANGE RD
GRANVILLE RD
BLACKWATER RD
JEVINGTON GDNS
COMPTON ST
WILMINGTON SQ
HARTINGTON PL
BURLINGTON PL
LASCELLES TER
HOWARD SQ
PEVENSEY RD
CEYLON PL
LEAF HALL RD
ST AUBYNS RD
REDOUBT RD
CAMBRIDGE RD
A259
A2021
EASTBOURNE
1
2
3
4
5
6
THE HOTEL

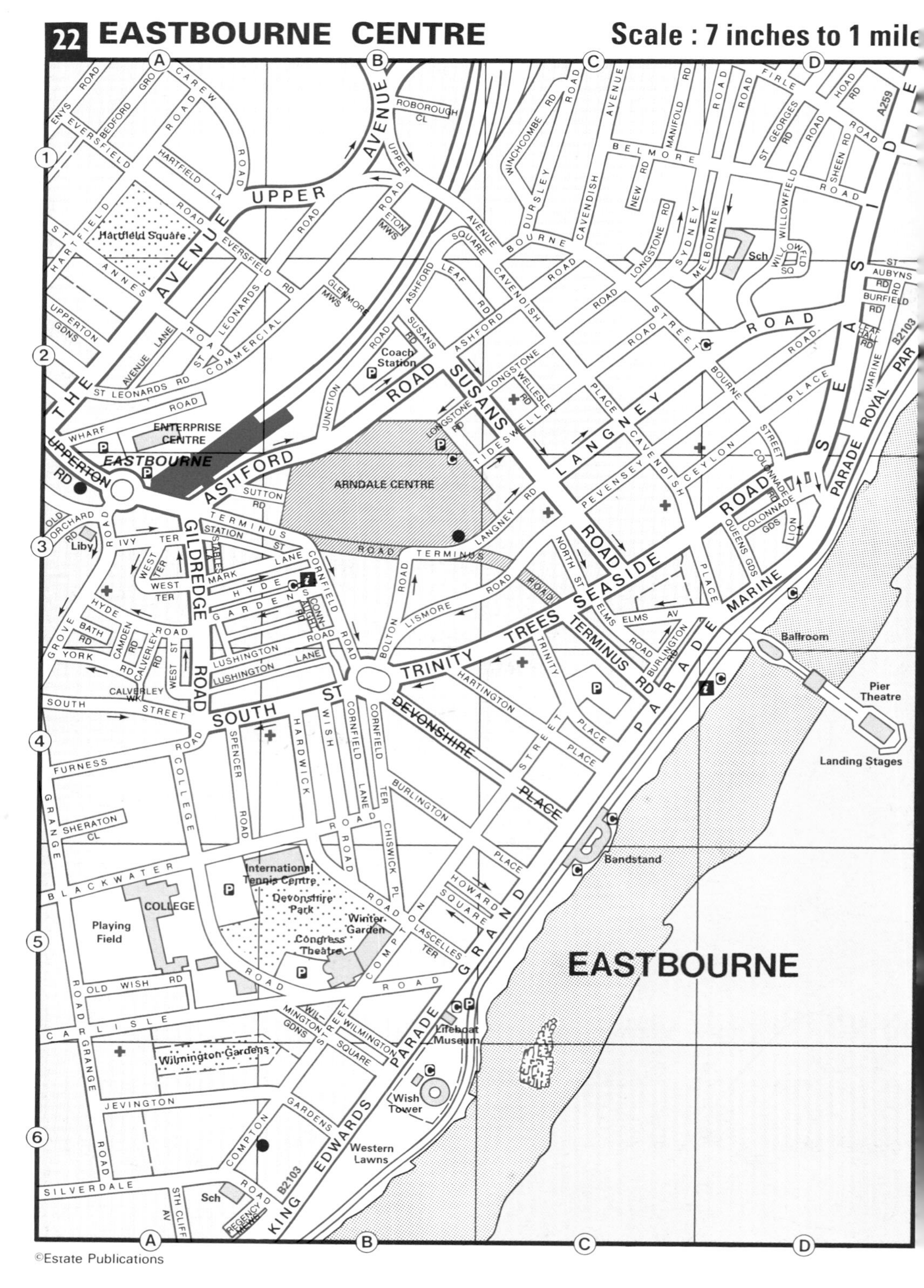

22
EASTBOURNE CENTRE
Scale : 7 inches to 1 mile
A
B
C
D
1
2
3
4
5
6
UPPER AVENUE
THE AVENUE
ROBOROUGH CL
UPPER AVENUE
Hartfield Square
HARTFIELD ROAD
HARTFIELD LA
EVERSFIELD ROAD
EVERSFIELD RD
BEDFORD GRO
CAREW ROAD
ENYS ROAD
ST ANNES ROAD
UPPERTON GDNS
ST LEONARDS ROAD
ST LEONARDS RD
AVENUE LANE
COMMERCIAL ROAD
WHARF ROAD
ENTERPRISE CENTRE
EASTBOURNE
UPPERTON RD
ASHFORD ROAD
ETON MWS
GLENMORE MWS
Coach Station
JUNCTION ROAD
ARNDALE CENTRE
SUTTON RD
TERMINUS ROAD
STATION ST
STABLES LA
ORCHARD RD
ORCHARD ROAD
Liby
IVY TER
WEST TER
GILDREDGE ROAD
MARK LANE
HYDE GARDENS
HYDE ROAD
CORNFIELD ROAD
GROVE ROAD
BATH RD
CAMDEN RD
CALVERLEY RD
CALVERLEY WK
YORK RD
WEST ST
LUSHINGTON ROAD
LUSHINGTON LANE
SOUTH STREET
SOUTH ST
TRINITY TREES
BOLTON ROAD
LISMORE ROAD
LANGNEY ROAD
SUSANS ROAD
LONGSTONE RD
TIDESWELL RD
WELLESLEY RD
WINCHCOMBE RD
DURSLEY RD
CAVENDISH AVENUE
CAVENDISH PLACE
BOURNE STREET
BELMORE ROAD
NEW RD
MANIFOLD RD
SYDNEY ROAD
MELBOURNE ROAD
FIRLE ROAD
ST GEORGES RD
WILLOWFIELD ROAD
WILLOWFIELD SQ
SHEEN RD
HOAD RD
A259
SEASIDE
Sch
ST AUBYNS RD
BURFIELD RD
LEAF HALL RD
MARINE RD
B2103
ROYAL PARADE
PEVENSEY RD
CEYLON PLACE
COLONNADE RD
COLONNADE GDNS
QUEENS GDS
LION
NORTH ST
SEASIDE ROAD
ELMS AV
ELMS RD
BURLINGTON RD
TERMINUS RD
TRINITY PLACE
MARINE PARADE
Ballroom
Pier Theatre
Landing Stages
HARTINGTON PLACE
DEVONSHIRE PLACE
BURLINGTON PLACE
CORNFIELD TER
CORNFIELD LANE
WISH ROAD
HARDWICK ROAD
SPENCER ROAD
COLLEGE ROAD
FURNESS ROAD
SHERATON CL
GRANGE ROAD
BLACKWATER ROAD
CHISWICK PL
HOWARD SQUARE
LASCELLES TER
GRAND PARADE
Bandstand
International Tennis Centre
Devonshire Park
Winter Garden
Congress Theatre
COLLEGE
Playing Field
COMPTON STREET
OLD WISH RD
CARLISLE ROAD
WILMINGTON GDNS
WILMINGTON SQUARE
Wilmington Gardens
Lifeboat Museum
Wish Tower
JEVINGTON GARDENS
COMPTON ROAD
KING EDWARDS PARADE
Western Lawns
SILVERDALE ROAD
STH CLIFF AV
REGENCY MEWS
EASTBOURNE
©Estate Publications

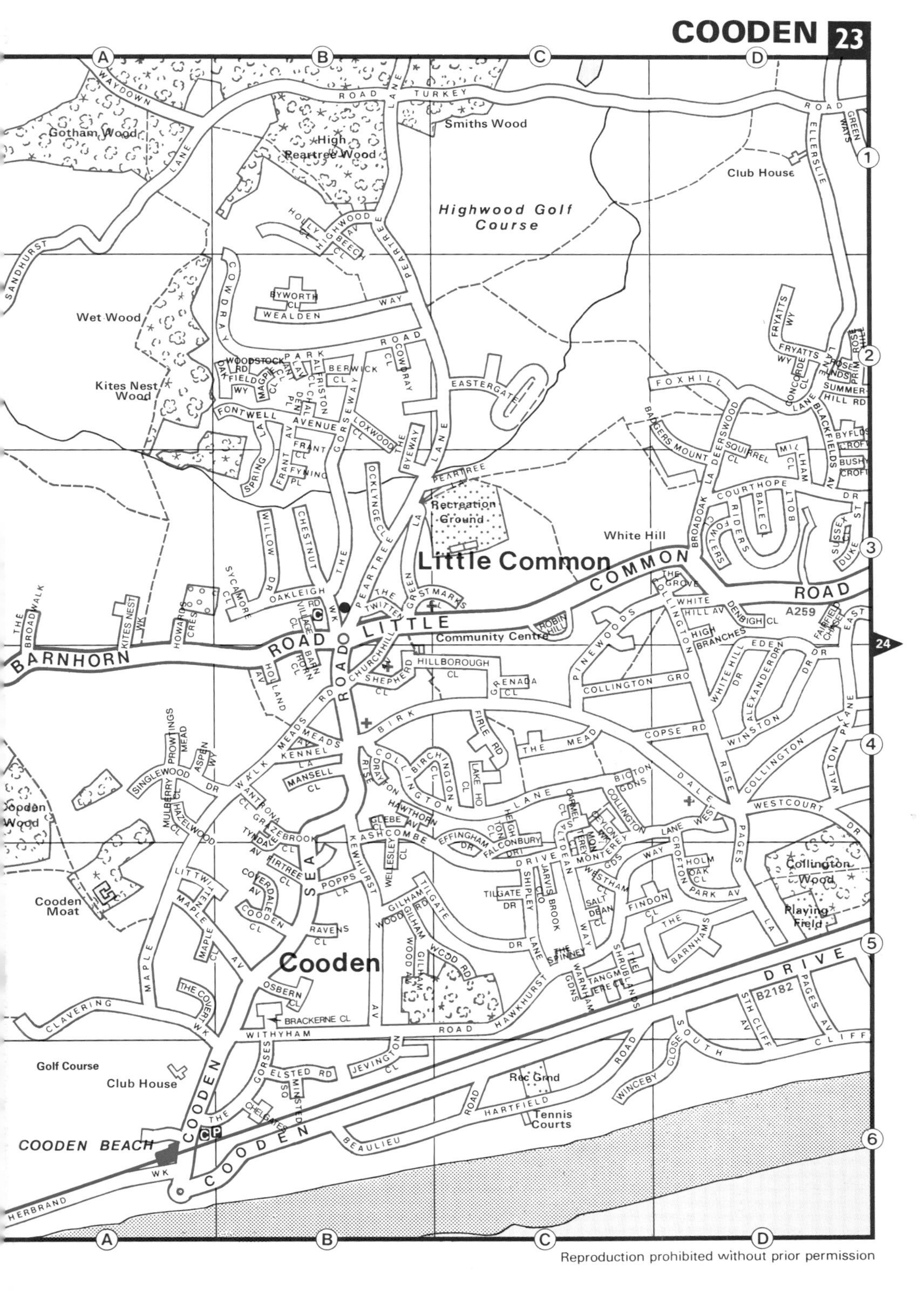
A
B
C
D
1
2
3
4
5
6
24
Gotham Wood
High Peartree Wood
Smiths Wood
Turkey Road
Waydown
Lane
Sandhurst
Highwood Golf Course
Club House
Ellerslie
Green Ways
Holly Cl
Highwood Av
Beech Cl
Peartree Lane
Byworth Cl
Wealden Way
Cowdray
Cowdray Park Road
Cowdray Cl
Wet Wood
Kites Nest Wood
Woodstock Rd
Oakfield Wy
Magpie Cl
Berwick Cl
Alfriston Cl
Fontwell Avenue
Eastergate
Gorseway
Loxwood Cl
The Byeway
Spring La
Frant Av
Frant Cl
Fyning Pl
Ocklynge Cl
Peartree La
Recreation Ground
Fryatts Way
Fryatts Wy
Concorde Cl
Foxhill
Badgers Mount
Deerswood La
Squirrel Cl
Milham Cl
Blackfields Av
Summerhill Rd
Byfleets Croft
Bush Croft
Courthope Dr
Broadoak La
Fowlers Cl
Riders
Bale Cl
Bolt Cl
Sussex St
Duke St
White Hill
Little Common
Little Common Road
A259
Willow Dr
Chestnut
Sycamore Cl
Oakleigh Rd
The Gorseway
Peartree
The Twitten
Green La
Grestmarks
The Broadwalk
Kites Nest Wk
Howards Cres
Village Cl
Barnhorn Road
Barn Hill
Holland Av
Church Hill
Shepherd Cl
Hillborough Cl
Community Centre
Robin Hill
The Grove
Collington
White Hill Av
Denbigh Cl
High Branches
Fairfield Chase
East
Pinewoods
Eden Dr
White Hill Dr
Alexander Dr
Collington Gro
Grenada Cl
Winston Dr
Birk Rd
Firle Rd
The Mead
Copse Rd
Walton Pk Lane
Meads Walk
Meads Av
Kennel La
Prowtings Mead
Aspen Way
Singlewood Dr
Mulberry Cl
Hazelwood
Cooden Wood
Mansell Cl
Collington Rise
Drayton Rise
Birchington Cl
Lake Ho
Collington Lane
Bicton Gdns
Dale Rise
Pages
Westcourt Dr
Antrona Cl
Glebe Av
Hawthorn Av
Grazebrook
Tyndale Av
Firtree Cl
Ashcombe
Effingham Dr
Heighton Cl
Falconbury Dr
Carmel
Ceylon
Monterey
Westham
West Lane
Crofton Park Av
Holm Oak Cl
Collington Wood
Playing Field
Littlwittene
Maple Cl
Coverdale Av
Cooden Cl
Sea Road
Popps La
Kewhurst
Wellesley Cl
Gilham Wood Rd
Tilgate
Tilgate Dr
Shipley Lane
Jarvis Brook Clo
Saltdean Cl
Findon Cl
Rottingdean
The Barnhams
Cooden Moat
Maple Av
Ravens Cl
Cooden
Osbern Cl
The Covert Wk
Wood Av
Wood Rd
The Spinney
Warnham Gdns
Tangmere Cl
The Shrublands
Hawkhurst
Drive
B2182
Pages Av
Sth Cliff Av
Cliff
Clavering Wk
Brackerne Cl
Withyham Road
Golf Course
Club House
Cooden
Gorses
Elsted Rd
Minsted Sq
Jevington Cl
Rec Grnd
South Close
Road
Winceby
Hartfield
Tennis Courts
The Chelgates
Cooden Beach
Cooden Drive
Beaulieu
Herbrand Wk
CP

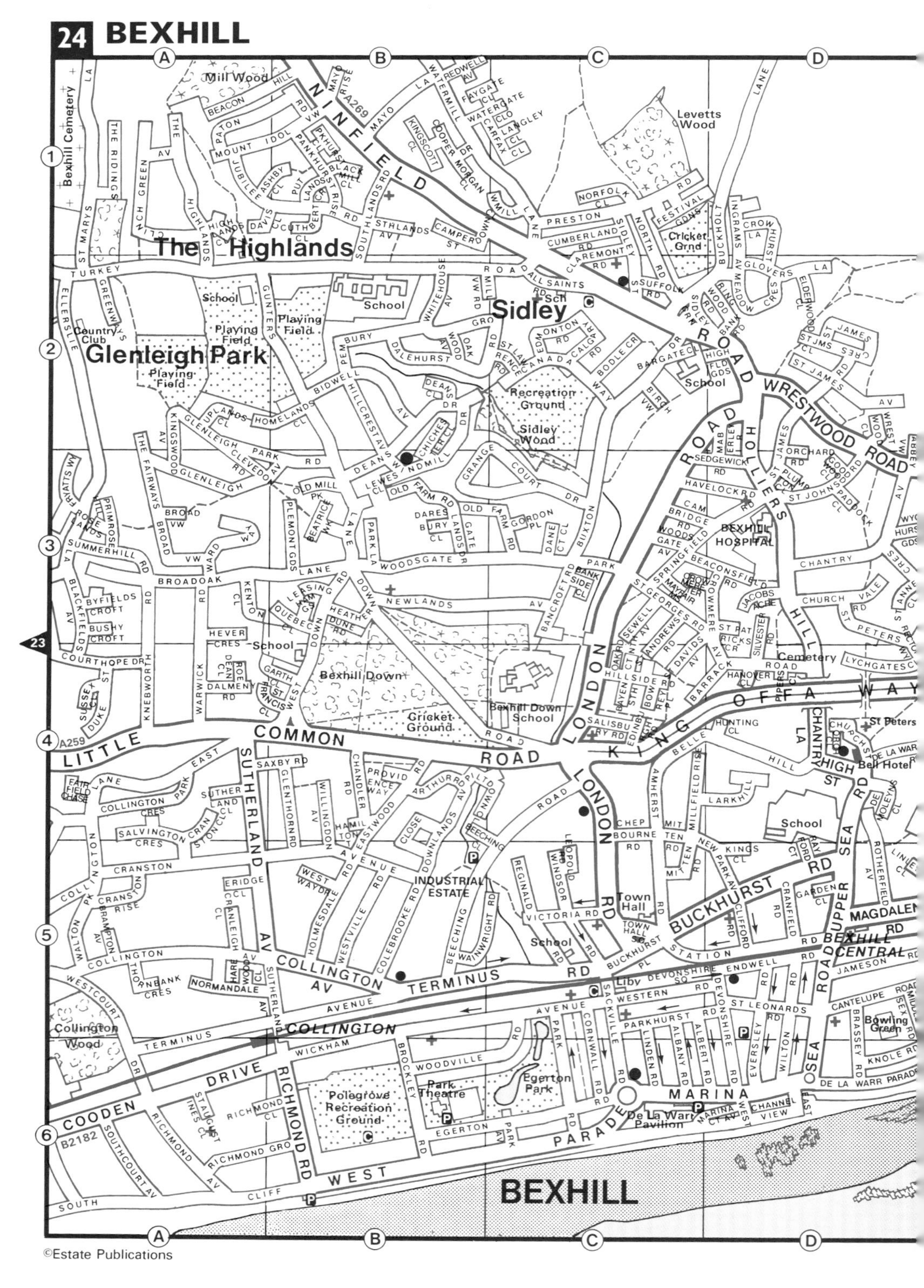
24
BEXHILL
The Highlands
Glenleigh Park
Sidley
Mill Wood
Levetts Wood
Bexhill Cemetery
Country Club
Playing Field
School
Recreation Ground
Sidley Wood
Cricket Grnd
BEXHILL HOSPITAL
Cemetery
Bexhill Down
Cricket Ground
Bexhill Down School
INDUSTRIAL ESTATE
Town Hall
Bell Hotel
St Peters
BEXHILL CENTRAL
COLLINGTON
Collington Wood
Polegrove Recreation Ground
Park Theatre
Egerton Park
De La Warr Pavilion
Bowling Green
NINFIELD ROAD
TURKEY ROAD
LITTLE COMMON ROAD
LONDON ROAD
KING OFFA WAY
WRESTWOOD ROAD
BUCKHURST RD
HOLLIERS HILL
SUTHERLAND AV
COLLINGTON AV
TERMINUS RD
TERMINUS AVENUE
COODEN DRIVE
RICHMOND RD
WEST PARADE
MARINA
SEA ROAD
UPPER SEA ROAD
WESTERN RD
DEVONSHIRE RD
ST LEONARDS RD
DE LA WARR PARADE
A269
A259
B2182
23
©Estate Publications

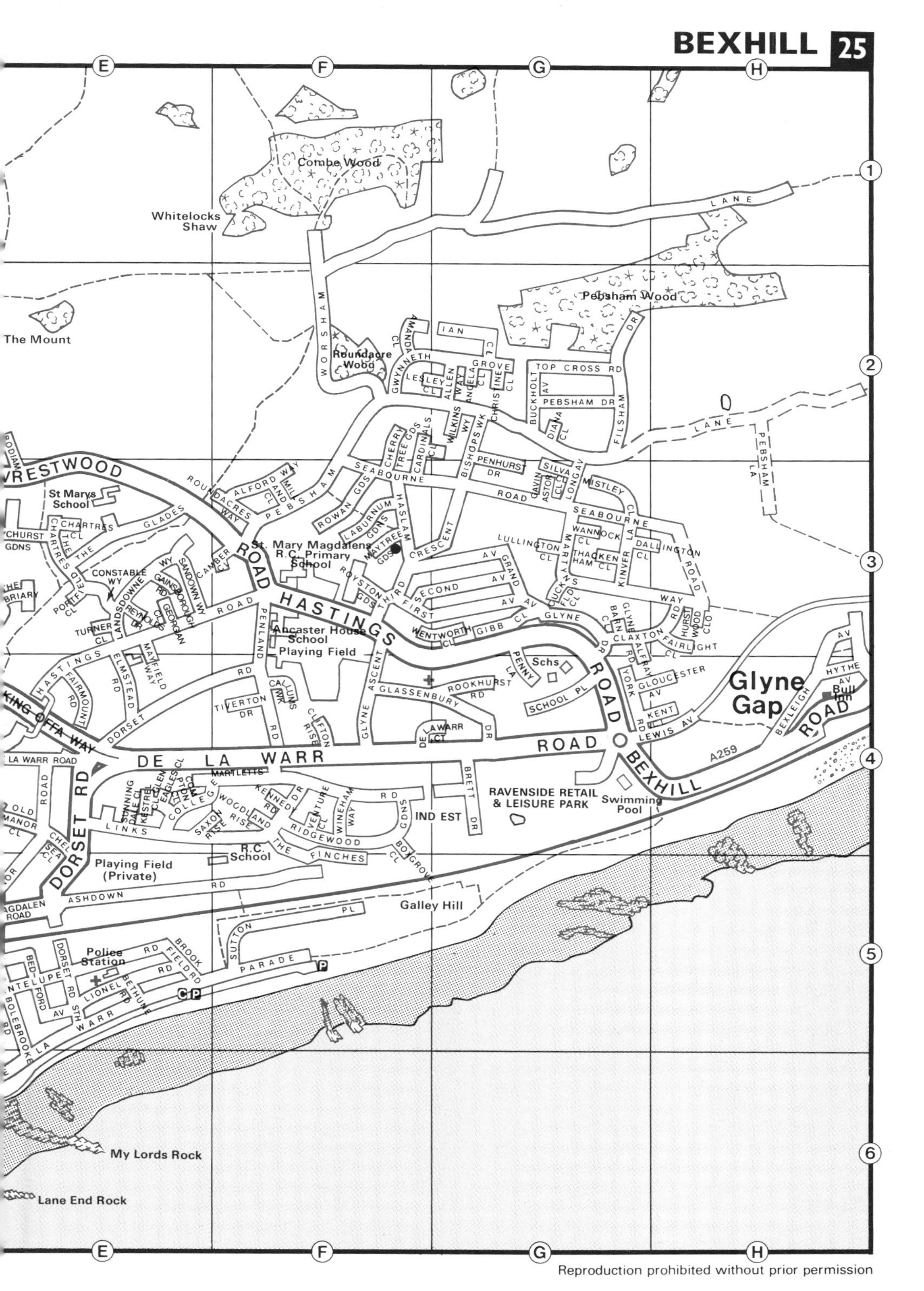

E   F   G   H

Combe Wood

Whitelocks Shaw

The Mount

Pebsham Wood

LANE

LANE

PEBSHAM LA

WORSHAM

Roundacre Wood

GWYNNETH

IAN

ANGELA CL

GROVE

CHRISTINE

TOP CROSS RD

PEBSHAM DR

FILSHAM DR

BUCKHOLT AV

LESLEY CL

ALLEN CL

WILKINS WY

BISHOPS WK

PENHURST DR

SILVA

MISTLEY CL

GAVIN

ASTON

CHERRY TREE GDNS

CARDINALS

SEABOURNE GDNS

LABURNUM GDNS

ROWAN GDNS

ALFORD WY

MILSHAM

PEBSHAM

ROUNDACRES WAY

HASLAM CRESCENT

WYTREE GDNS

SEABOURNE ROAD

SEABOURNE CLOSE

WANNOCK CL

THACKERAY CL

DALLINGTON CLOSE

MARTYRS

LULLINGTON CL

KINVER

WRESTWOOD

St Marys School

CHARTRES CL

CHARTRES GDNS

THE GLADES

CONSTABLE WY

GAINSBOROUGH

SANDOWN WY

PORTEY

LANDSDOWNE RD

REYNOLDS

OLD GEORGIAN

TURNER CL

THE BRIARY

CAMBER

ROAD

HASTINGS ROAD

ST MARY MAGDALENS R.C. PRIMARY SCHOOL

ROYSTON CL

POST

FIRST

CRESCENT

SECOND AV

THIRD AV

GRAND AV

LUCKHURST

CLAXTON RD

GLYNE ROAD

GIBB CL

WENTWORTH CL

Ancaster House School Playing Field

PENLAND RD

TIVERTON DR

CALUNS MK

CLIFTON RISE

GLYNE ASCENT

GLASSENBURY

ROOKHURST RD

PENNY CL

SCHOOL PL

Schs

DE LA WARR CT

GLYNE AV

KENT AV

GLOUCESTER AV

LEWIS AV

BARN RISE

FAIRLIGHT RD

HURST RD

WOOD RD

GLYNLEIGH

BEXLEIGH AV

HYTHE AV

Glyne Gap

Bull Inn

A259

ROAD BEXHILL

ROAD

KING OFFA WAY

DE LA WARR ROAD

FAIRMOUNT RD

EMSTEAD RD

MAYFIELD WY

DORSET CL

LA WARR ROAD

DORSET RD

OLD MANOR CL

MAGDALEN ROAD

CHEL

ASHDOWN RD

LINKS

STANNING

DALE CL

KESTREL CL

EAGLES CL

BEXHILL COLLEGE

SAXON RISE

KENNEDY CL

WOODLAND

VENTURE RD

WINEHAM WAY

RIDGEWOOD

BRETT DR

BOLGROVE

WINEHAM CL

IND EST

RAVENSIDE RETAIL & LEISURE PARK

Swimming Pool

R.C. School

THE FINCHES

MARTLETS

Playing Field (Private)

Galley Hill

PL

SUTTON RD

PARADE

Police Station

BED FORD RD

DORSET RD

BROOK RD

FIELD RD

BETHUNE

LIONEL RD

ANTELUPE RD

BOLEBROOKE RD

LA WARR RD

My Lords Rock

Lane End Rock

1 2 3 4 5 6

E   F   G   H

The Index includes some names for which there is insufficient space on the maps. These names are preceded by an * and are followed by the nearest adjoining thoroughfare.

BEXHILL

St James Rd. TN40 24 D3
St Johns Rd. TN40 24 D3
St Lawrence Rd. TN39 24 C2
St Leonards Rd. TN40 24 D5
St Marks Clo. TN39 23 B3
St Marys La. TN39 24 A1
St Patricks Cres. TN40 24 D3
St Peters Cres. TN40 24 D3
Salisbury Rd. TN40 24 C4
Saltdean Clo. TN39 23 C5
Saltdean Way. TN39 23 C4
Salvington Cres. TN39 24 A4
Sandhurst La. TN39 23 B2
Sandown Way. TN40 25 E3
Saxby Rd. TN39 24 B4
Saxon Rise. TN40 25 E4
School Pl. TN40 25 G4
Sea Rd. TN40 24 D6
Seabourne Rd. TN40 25 F3
Second Av. TN40 25 F3
Sedgewick Rd. TN40 24 C3
Sewell Av. TN40 24 C3
Shepherd Clo. TN39 23 B4
Shipley La. TN39 23 C5
Sidley Grn. TN39 24 C2
Sidley St. TN39 24 C1
Silva Clo. TN40 25 G3
Silvester Rd. TN40 24 D4
Singlewood Dri. TN39 23 A4
South Cliff Av. TN39 23 D5
South Cliff. TN39 24 A6
Southcourt Av. TN39 24 A6
Southlands Av. TN39 24 B1
Southlands Rd. TN39 24 B1
Spindlewood Dr. TN39 23 A4
Spring La. TN39 23 B3
Springfield Rd. TN39 24 C3
Squirrel Clo. TN39 23 D2
Station Rd. TN40 24 C5
Suffolk Rd. TN39 24 C2
Summerhill Rd. TN39 24 A3
Sunningdale Clo. TN40 25 E4
Sussex Clo. TN39 24 A4
Sutherland Ave. TN39 24 A4
Sutherland Rd. TN39 24 A4
Sutton Pl. TN40 25 F5
Sycamore Clo. TN39 23 B3

Tangmere Clo. TN39 23 C5
Terminus Av. TN39 24 A6
Terminus Rd. TN39 24 B5
Thakeham Clo. TN40 25 G3
The Barnhams. TN39 23 D5
The Briary. TN40 25 E3
The Broadwalk. TN39 23 A3
The Byeway. TN39 23 B2
The Covert. TN39 23 A5
The Fairways. TN39 24 A2
The Finches. TN39 25 F4
The Glades. TN40 25 E3
The Gorses. TN39 23 A6
The Gorseway. TN39 23 B3
The Grove. TN39 23 D3
The Highlands. TN39 24 A1
The Mead. TN39 23 C4
The Ridings. TN39 24 A1
The Shrublands. TN39 23 C5
The Spinney. TN39 23 C5
The Twitten. TN39 23 B3
Third Av. TN40 25 F3
Thornbank Cres. TN39 24 A5
Tilgate Dri. TN39 23 C5
Tiverton Dri. TN40 25 F4
Top Cross Rd. TN39 25 G2
Town Hall Sq. TN39 24 C5
Turkey Rd. TN39 24 A2
Turner Rd. TN40 25 E3
Tyndale Rd. TN39 23 B4

Uplands Clo. . TN39 24 A5
Upper Sea Rd. TN40 24 D5

Venture Clo. TN40 25 F4
Village Clo. TN39 23 B3
Victoria Rd. TN39 24 C5

Wainwright Rd. TN39 24 B5
Walton Pk. TN39 24 A4
Wannock Clo. TN40 25 G3
Ward Way. TN39 24 A3
Warnham Gdns. TN39 23 C5
Warwick Rd. TN39 24 A4
Watergate. TN39 24 B1
Watermill Clo. TN39 24 C1
Watermill La. TN39 24 B1
Wealden Way. TN39 23 B2

Wellesley Clo. TN39 23 B5
Wentworth Clo. TN40 25 F3
West Down Rd. TN39 24 B4
West Parade. TN39 24 B6
Westcourt Dri. TN39 24 A5
Western Rd. TN40 24 C5
Westham Clo. TN39 23 C5
Westville Rd. TN39 24 B5
Westway Dri. TN39 24 B5
White Hill Av. TN39 23 D3
White Hill Dri. TN39 23 D4
Whitehouse Av. TN39 24 B2
Whydown Rd. TN39 23 A1
Wickham Av. TN39 24 B6
Wilkins Way. TN39 25 G2
Willingdon Av. TN39 24 B4
Willow Dri. TN39 23 B3
Wilton Rd. TN40 24 D6
Winceby Clo. TN39 23 D6
Windmill Dri. TN39 24 B3
Windsor Rd. TN39 24 C5
Wineham Way. TN40 25 F4
Winston Dri. TN39 23 D4
Withyham Rd. TN39 23 B5
Woodland Rise. TN40 25 F4
Woodsgate Av. TN40 24 C3
Woodsgate Pk. TN39 24 B3
Woodstock Rd. TN39 23 B2
Woodville Rd. TN39 24 B6
Worsham La. TN40 25 F2
Wrestwood Clo. TN40 24 D2
Wrestwood Rd. TN40 24 D2
Wychurst Gdns. TN40 24 D3

York Rd. TN40 25 G4

EASTBOURNE

Aberdale Rd. BN26 11 E3
Acacia Rd. BN22 17 F1
Addingham Rd. BN22 21 H1
Adur Dri. BN24 12 C2
Albert Pl. BN26 10 C2
Albert Rd. BN26 10 C2
Albert Ter. BN21 20 B1
Albion Rd. BN22 21 G1
Alder Clo. BN23 18 C3
Alexandra Rd. BN22 19 E5
Alfred Rd. BN23 19 F3
Alfriston Clo. BN20 20 C3
Allfrey Rd. BN22 18 D5
Alverstone Clo. BN23 12 C3
Amberley Rd. BN22 17 E2
Anchorage Way. BN23 19 H1
Anderida Rd. BN26 10 D6
Angus Clo. BN24 16 D2
Annington Rd. BN22 18 C6
Anson Clo. BN23 19 F4
Appledore Clo. BN23 13 E5
Arkwright Rd. BN23 18 B2
Arlington Rd. BN21 21 E2
Arun Clo. BN24 12 B2
Arun Way. BN24 12 B2
Arundel Clo. BN24 15 G3
Arundel Rd. BN21 21 E2
Ascham Pl. BN20 20 D4
Ascot Clo. BN20 21 E5
Ash Clo. BN22 11 G6
Ash Gro. BN24 13 F1
Ashburnham Gdns.
   BN21 20 D1
Ashburnham Rd. BN21 20 D1
Ashford Rd. BN21 22 A3
Ashford Sq. BN21 22 A3
Ashgate Rd. BN23 13 F5
Ashington Rd. BN22 12 C6
Aspen Rd. BN22 17 F1
Astaire Av. BN22 18 B6
Athelstan Clo. BN23 19 F3
Atlantic Dri. BN23 19 G4
Attfield Walk. BN22 12 B4
Austen Walk. BN23 13 F5
Avard Cres. BN20 16 D5
Avenue La. BN21 22 A2
Avondale Rd. BN22 21 G1
Aylesbury Av. BN23 19 F3
Ayscue Clo. BN23 19 G4

Babylon Way. BN20 16 D3
Badgers Brow. BN20 16 D3
Badlesmere Rd. BN22 18 B5
Bahram Rd. BN26 10 B3
Bailey Cres. BN22 10 D6

Baillie Av. BN22 18 C6
Bakers Rd. BN21 20 D2
Bakewell Rd. BN21 20 C1
Baldwin Av. BN21 17 E5
Banner Way. BN24 12 D1
Barcombe Clo. BN20 20 B2
Barcombe Walk. BN20 20 B2
Barden Rd. BN22 21 H1
Barming Clo. BN23 13 E5
Barn Clo. BN24 12 C1
Barnham Clo. BN22 12 B5
Barons Way. BN26 10 B4
Barrie Clo. BN23 13 E5
Barrier Reef Way. BN23 19 G2
Bartley Mill Clo. BN24 12 D2
Baslow Rd. BN20 20 C6
Bath Rd. BN21 22 A3
Bathford Clo. BN23 13 E5
Bay Av. BN24 15 F4
Bay Pond Rd. BN21 20 D2
Bay Rd. BN24 15 F5
Bay Tree La. BN26 10 B1
Bayham Rd. BN22 21 H2
Beach Rd. BN22 18 D6
Beachy Head Rd. BN20 20 B6
Beachlands Way. BN24 15 H3
Beamsley Rd. BN22 21 H1
Beatrice La. BN21 21 E2
Beatty Rd. BN23 19 F5
Beaulieu Dri. BN24 12 C2
Bedford Gro. BN21 22 A1
Bedford Well Rd. BN22 21 F1
Beechfield Clo. BN24 12 D1
Beechwood Cres. BN20 20 D2
Beechy Av. BN20 20 B1
Beechy Gdns. BN20 20 B1
Beggars La. BN24 12 D2
Bellevue Rd. BN22 18 D6
Belmore Rd. BN22 22 C1
Beltring Rd. BN22 21 G1
Beltring Ter. BN22 21 G1
*Belvedere Ct,
   St Annes Rd. BN20 21 E1
Bembridge Rd. BN23 12 C4
Benbow Av. BN23 19 F5
Benjamin Clo. BN20 12 B5
Beristede Clo. BN20 21 E4
Berkeley Walk. BN23 13 F4
Bermuda Pl. BN23 19 G4
Bernards La. BN21 21 E2
Bernhard Gdns. BN20 10 C4
Berwick Clo. BN22 11 F6
Beverington Dri. BN21 17 E5
Beverington Rd. BN21 17 E5
Bexhill Rd. BN22 18 D5
Biddenden Clo. BN23 13 F5
Binsted Clo. BN20 17 F2
Birch Clo. BN23 18 D4
Birch Rd. BN23 18 D4
Birling St. BN21 20 C1
*Biscay Av,
   Viking Way. BN23 19 F3
Black Path Rd. BN26 10 C3
Blackthorn Clo. BN23 17 F1
Blackwater Rd. BN20 22 A5
Blakes Way. BN23 19 F5
Blatchington Mill Dri.
   BN24 12 D2
Blenheim Way. BN26 11 F3
Bodiam Cres. BN22 12 B5
Bodmin Clo. BN20 20 B2
Bolsover Rd. BN20 21 E5
Bolton Rd. BN21 22 B4
Boniface Clo. BN24 12 D1
Borough La. BN20 20 D2
Borrowdale Clo. BN23 12 C4
Boscawen Rd. BN23 19 G4
Boship Clo. BN23 12 C3
Boswell Walk. BN23 13 F5
Boston Clo. BN23 19 G4
Bourne St. BN21 22 C1
Bowood Av. BN22 18 C5
Bracken Rd. BN20 16 C6
Bradford St. BN21 20 C2
Brading Clo. BN23 12 C3
Bramble Clo. BN23 12 D4
Bramley Rd. BN26 11 F3
Brampton Rd. BN22 12 B6
Brand Rd. BN21 17 G2
Branston Rd. BN22 17 F2
Brassey Av. BN22 12 B5
Brede Clo. BN23 19 E5
Brendon Clo. BN23 13 F3
Briar Pl. BN23 12 D4
Bridge End. BN24 14 D3
Bridgemere Rd. BN22 18 B6

Brightland Rd. BN20 20 C2
Brightling Rd. BN26 10 C4
Britten Clo. BN23 13 F4
Broad Oak Clo. BN24 12 B3
Broad Rd. BN20 10 B6
Broadview Clo. BN20 10 C5
Broadwater Way. BN23 18 A3
Brocks Ghyll. BN22 10 C6
Brodie Pl. BN21 20 D2
Brodrick Clo. BN22 17 G2
Brodrick Rd. BN22 17 F1
Bromley Clo. BN23 13 E5
Brook St. BN26 10 C3
Brookland Clo. BN24 15 G3
Brookmead Clo. BN20 18 C6
Brookside Av. BN26 10 C3
Broom Clo. BN22 17 F1
Broomfield St. BN21 20 B2
Brown Jack Av. BN26 10 B3
Browning Walk. BN23 13 F5
Brydges Clo. BN22 18 C5
Buckhurst Clo. BN20 16 D3
Burfield Rd. BN22 22 D2
Burleigh Pl. BN22 18 D5
Burlington Pl. BN21 22 B4
Burlington Rd. BN21 22 C4
Burlow Clo. BN22 11 E6
Burnside. BN26 10 D3
Burrow Down. BN20 16 C6
Burrow Down Clo.
   BN20 16 C6
Burton Rd. BN21 17 F5
Buttermere Way. BN23 12 D3
Butts La. BN20 16 B3
Buxton Rd. BN20 20 D5
Byland Clo. BN21 22 B4
Byron Walk. BN23 13 F4

Cabot Clo. BN23 19 G5
Caburn Clo. BN24 12 B3
Cade St. BN22 12 B5
Cairngorm Clo. BN23 19 E4
Calverley Rd. BN21 22 A4
*Calverley Walk,
   Calverley Rd. BN21 22 A4
Camber Clo. BN24 15 G3
Camber Dri. BN24 15 G3
Camber Way. BN24 15 G3
Cambridge Rd. BN22 21 H2
Camden Rd. BN21 22 A4
Canterbury Clo. BN22 16 D1
Canute Clo. BN23 19 F3
Carew Rd. BN21 21 E1
Carisbrooke Clo. BN23 12 C3
Carlisle Rd. BN21 20 C5
Carlton Rd. BN22 21 H1
Carroll Walk. BN23 13 F5
Castle Bolton. BN23 13 E3
Castle Dri. BN24 15 E5
Castle Rd. BN24 13 H1
Castle View Gdns. BN24 13 F1
Castleross Rd. BN24 15 E5
Catsfield Clo. BN24 12 B3
Cavalry Cres. BN20 16 D6
Cavendish Pl. BN21 22 C1
Cavendish Pl. BN21 22 C2
Cedar Clo. BN22 17 E1
Central Av. BN20 16 D6
Central Av. BN26 10 D3
Ceylon Pl. BN21 22 C3
Chaffinch Rd. BN23 13 E5
Chailey Clo. BN20 20 B2
Chalk Farm Clo. BN20 16 D2
Chalvinton Rd. BN21 17 E4
Chamberlain Rd. BN21 20 C1
Channel View Rd. BN22 18 D6
Channelview Rd. BN24 15 F4
Charleston Rd. BN21 20 C1
Chatfield Cres. BN22 17 E2
Chatsworth Gdns.
   BN20 21 E5
Chaucer Walk. BN23 13 F4
Chawbrook Rd. BN22 21 G1
Chelworth Rd. BN22 17 E1
Cherry Garden Rd.
   BN20 20 B2
Cherwell Clo. BN24 12 B2
Chesterfield Gdns.
   BN21 21 E5
Chesterfield Rd. BN20 20 D5
Chestnut Dri. BN26 10 D3
Cheviot Clo. BN23 13 F3
Chilham Clo. BN23 13 E5
Chiltern Clo. BN23 13 A3
Chiltern Ct. BN26 10 C2

Chiswick Pl. BN21 22 B4
Church Av. BN24 13 H1
Church Bailey. BN24 14 C4
Church Clo. BN20 10 C5
Church La. BN21 20 D2
Church La. BN24 14 D3
Church Rd. BN26 10 C3
Church St,
   Old Town. BN20 20 C2
Church St,
   Willingdon. BN20 16 D2
Churchdale Av. BN22 18 C5
Churchdale Pl. BN22 18 C5
Churchdale Rd. BN22 18 C5
Churchill Clo. BN20 20 D2
Chyngton Clo. BN23 12 C3
Clarence Rd. BN22 21 G1
Claytin Mill Rd. BN24 12 D2
Claxton Clo. BN21 17 F6
Cleevelands. BN22 16 D1
Clement La. BN26 10 C4
Cleveland Clo. BN23 13 E4
Cliff Rd. BN20 20 D6
Clifford Av. BN21 17 E5
Clifton Clo. BN22 17 F3
Close Eight. BN23 13 F4
Close Eighteen. BN23 13 F5
Close Eleven. BN23 13 G4
Close Fifteen. BN23 13 F5
Close Five. BN23 13 F4
Close Four. BN23 13 F4
Close Fourteen. BN23 13 G4
Close Nine. BN23 13 G5
Close Nineteen. BN23 13 F5
Close One. BN23 13 F5
Close Seven. BN23 13 F4
Close Seventeen. BN23 13 F4
Close Six. BN23 13 F4
Close Sixteen. BN23 13 F5
Close Ten. BN23 13 G5
Close Three. BN23 13 F5
Close Twelve. BN23 13 G4
Close Twenty. BN23 13 F5
Close Twentyfive. BN23 13 F5
Close Twentyfour.
   BN23 13 F5
Close Two. BN23 13 F5
Cobald Rd. BN24 15 G4
Cobbold Av. BN21 17 E5
Cochrane Clo. BN23 19 E4
Coleridge Walk. BN23 13 F4
College Grn. BN21 20 D1
College Rd. BN21 22 A4
Collier Clo. BN22 18 C4
Collier Clo. BN24 15 F5
Collington Clo. BN23 21 E5
Collingwood Clo. BN23 19 F5
Colonnade Gdns.
   BN21 22 D3
Colonnade Rd. BN21 22 D3
Colt Stocks Rd. BN20 20 D5
Columbus Dri. BN23 19 G5
Colwood Cres. BN20 16 D6
Command Rd. BN20 16 D6
Commercial Rd. BN21 22 A2
Compton Dri. BN20 20 B3
Compton Place Rd.
   BN20 20 D2
Compton St. BN21 22 B5
Coniston Rd. BN23 13 E3
Connaught Rd. BN21 22 B3
Constable Rd. BN23 13 F6
Cook Av. BN23 19 F5
Coombe La. BN20 20 C6
Coombe Rise. BN20 16 C1
Coombe Road. BN20 20 B1
Coopers Hill. BN20 16 D1
Coppice Av. BN20 10 C5
Coppice Clo. BN20 10 C5
Coral Reef Clo. BN23 19 G2
Cormorant Clo. BN23 12 D5
Cornfield La. BN21 22 B4
Cornfield Rd. BN21 22 B3
Cornfield Ter. BN21 22 B4
Cornish Clo. BN23 12 D3
Cornmill Gdns. BN26 10 B5
Cornwallis Clo. BN23 19 F4
Cotswold Clo. BN23 13 E3
Court Rd. BN22 12 B5
Courtland Rd. BN23 10 D4
Courtlands Rd. BN22 18 B6
Cranborne Av. BN20 20 B5
Crawley Cres. BN22 17 G1
Cresta Clo. BN23 10 D2
Croft Clo. BN26 10 C5

Milbrook Gdns. BN20 16 D5
Milfoil Dri. BN23 12 D4
Mill Clo. BN26 10 B5
Mill Gap Rd. BN21 21 E1
Mill Rd. BN21 20 D1
Mill Way. BN26 10 B5
Millstream Gdns. BN26 10 B5
Millview Clo. BN24 13 E1
Millward Rd. BN24 15 E6
Milnthorpe Rd. BN20 20 D5
Milton Cres. BN21 20 C1
Milton Rd. BN21 20 B1
Milton St. BN24 12 C1
Mimosa Clo. BN26 10 C2
Mimram Rd. BN24 12 C2
Minster Clo. BN26 10 C2
Moat Croft Rd. BN21 20 D2
Mona Rd. BN22 21 G1
Monarch Gdns. BN23 19 F2
Monceux Rd. BN21 20 C1
Montague Way. BN24 13 G2
Montford Clo. BN24 13 G1
Montford Rd. BN24 13 G1
Mortain Rd. BN24 13 G1
Mortimer Gdns. BN26 10 B5
Mortimer Rd. BN22 18 B5
Motcombe La. BN21 20 D1
Motcombe Rd. BN21 20 C2
Mount Rd. BN20 21 E5
Mountbatten Dri. BN23 19 F4
Mountfield Rd. BN22 12 B6
Mountney Dri. BN24 15 G3
Mountney Gardens Business. Pk. BN23 13 H3
Mountney Rd. BN21 20 C1
Moy Av. BN22 18 B6
Mulberry Clo. BN22 11 G6
Myrtle Rd. BN22 19 E5

Naomi Clo. BN20 20 D4
Nelson Dri. BN23 19 F5
Netherfield Av. BN23 13 G5
Nevill Av. BN22 17 G2
Neville Rd. BN22 21 G1
Nightingale Clo. BN23 12 D5
New College Clo. BN23 12 D3
New Pl. BN21 20 C2
New Rd. BN22 22 C1
New Rd. BN26 10 D3
New Upperton Rd. BN21 20 D2
Newick Rd. BN20 16 D5
Norman Rd. BN24 15 E5
North Av. BN20 16 D6
North Clo. BN26 10 D2
North Rd. BN24 15 E5
North St. BN21 22 C3
Northbourne Rd. BN22 18 C5
Northern Av. BN26 10 D2
Northfield. BN26 10 B4
Northiam Rd. BN21 20 B1
Norway Rd. BN22 18 D5
Nursery Clo. BN26 10 D3
Nutbourne Clo. BN23 13 G5
Nuthatch Rd. BN23 12 D4
Nutley Mill Rd. BN24 12 D2

Oak Tree La. BN23 12 D3
Oaklands Park. BN24 13 F1
Oaklands Clo. BN26 10 D3
Oakleaf Dri. BN26 10 C2
Ocklynge Av. BN21 20 D1
Ocklynge Rd. BN21 20 D1
Offham Clo. BN24 12 B3
Okehurst Rd. BN21 20 C2
Old Barn Clo. BN20 16 D2
Old Camp Rd. BN20 20 B3
Old Drive. BN26 10 C3
Old Drove. BN23 13 E4
Old Mansion Clo. BN20 16 C3
Old Mill La. BN26 10 B6
Old Motcombe Mews. BN21 20 C2
Old Orchard Rd. BN21 21 E3
Old School Clo. BN26 10 C2
Old Wish Rd. BN21 22 A5
Oldfield Av. BN20 10 C5
Oldfield Rd. BN20 10 C5
*Orchard Par, The Triangle. BN20 10 D6
Orchid Clo. BN23 12 D4
Orwell Clo. BN24 12 C2
Osbourne Rd. BN20 20 B2
Otham Court La. BN26 10 C1
Otham Rd. BN22 12 B5
Otteham Clo. BN26 10 D3
Oulton Clo. BN23 12 D3
Oxendean Clo. BN22 10 D5
Oxendean Gdns. BN22 10 D5
Oxford Rd. BN22 21 G1

Pacific Dri. BN23 19 G2
Paddock Gdns. BN26 10 B5
Pagham Clo. BN23 12 C3
Palliser Clo. BN23 19 F5
Palma Clo. BN26 10 C2
Paradise Clo. BN20 20 C3
Paradise Dri. BN20 20 C4
Park Av. BN21 17 E4
Park Clo. BN20 20 D2
Park Croft. BN26 10 C5
Park La. BN21 17 E3
Parker Clo. BN21 17 F6
Parkfield Av. BN22 17 F2
Parkway. BN20 16 C3
Parry Clo. BN23 13 F4
Parsonage Rd. BN21 20 C2
Pashley Rd. BN20 20 B3
Patcham Mill Rd. BN24 12 D2
Pebble Rd. BN24 15 G4
Peelings La. BN24 12 C1
Pelham Clo. BN24 13 G2
Pembury Rd. BN23 13 E6
Penhale Rd. BN22 18 D6
Penhurst Clo. BN22 12 C6
Pennine Way. BN23 13 E3
Penrith Way. BN23 12 D3
Pensford Dri. BN23 13 E4
Pentland Clo. BN23 13 F4
Peppercombe Rd. BN20 20 B2
Pepys Walk. BN23 13 F4
Percival Cres. BN22 12 A4
Percival Rd. BN22 12 A5
Petworth Pl. BN22 17 G1
Pevensey Bay Rd. BN23 13 G6
Pevensey Park Rd. BN24 13 G1
Pevensey Rd. BN21 22 C3
Pevensey Rd. BN26 10 D3
Peyton Clo. BN23 19 F4
Phoenix Dri. BN23 19 H3
Piltdown Way. BN24 12 B3
Pinewood Clo. BN22 17 E1
Pitcairn Av. BN23 19 H1
Plover Clo. BN23 13 E5
Plumpton Clo. BN23 12 C3
Plymouth Clo. BN23 19 F3
Pococks Rd. BN21 17 F6
Polgate By-Pass. BN26 10 B1
Poplar Walk. BN22 11 F6
Port Rd. BN22 12 B6
Porters Way. BN26 10 D3
Portsdown Way. BN20 16 C1
Potts Marsh Ind Est. BN23 13 G3
Pound Clo. BN23 19 F5
Prideaux Rd. BN21 17 F6
Primrose Clo. BN23 12 D4
Prince William Par. BN23 19 F5
Princes Rd. BN23 19 E5
Priory Clo. BN24 15 F4
Priory Heights. BN20 16 C6
Priory La. BN23 13 G4
Priory Orchard. BN23 13 F6
Priory Rd. BN23 13 F6
Prospect Gdns. BN21 20 D1
Pulborough Av. BN22 17 G2
Purbeck Clo. BN23 13 E3

Quantock Clo. BN23 13 E4
Quebec Clo. BN23 19 F4
Queens Cres. BN23 19 E4
Queens Gdns. BN21 22 D3
Queens Rd. BN23 19 E4

Raleigh Clo. BN23 19 F5
Ramsay Way. BN23 19 F4
Rangemore Dri. BN21 17 F4
Ranworth Clo. BN23 12 D3
Rapsons Rd. BN20 10 C6
Rattle Rd. BN24 12 C2
Ratton Dri. BN20 16 D4
Ratton Rd. BN21 20 D1
Ravenscroft. BN20 21 E5
Rectory Clo. BN20 20 C2
Redford Clo. BN23 13 F5
*Redman King Ho, Granville Rd. BN21 21 E2
Redoubt Rd. BN22 21 H1
Reedham Rd. BN23 12 D3
Regency Mews. BN20 22 A6
Regnum Clo. BN22 11 G5
Reynolds Rd. BN23 13 F6
Reynolds Town La. BN26 10 B3
Richmond Pl. BN21 21 E2
Richmond Rd. BN24 15 F4
Ridgelands Clo. BN20 20 B3
Ringmer Way. BN23 12 C3
Ringwood Clo. BN22 18 B6
Ringwood Rd. BN22 18 B5
Ripsley Clo. BN23 13 F5
Rise Park Gdns. BN23 13 F5
Robin Clo. BN23 12 D5
Roborough Clo. BN21 22 B1
Rochester Clo. BN20 20 B5
Rockall Av. BN23 19 F3
Rockhurst Dri. BN20 16 D5
Rodmill Dri. BN21 17 F6
Rodmill Rd. BN21 17 F6
Rodney Clo. BN23 19 F4
Roffrey Av. BN22 17 F2
*Roman Croft, Selwyn Rd. BN21 20 D1
Romans Way. BN24 13 F1
Romney Rd. BN26 11 E3
Romney St. BN22 18 D6
Rosebery Av. BN22 17 G2
Rosedale Pl. BN22 11 F6
Roselands Av. BN22 18 C5
Roselands Clo. BN22 18 C6
Rosetti Rd. BN24 15 E5
Roseveare Rd. BN22 18 C5
Rother Av. BN24 12 B2
Rotherfield Av. BN23 12.B3
Rotunda Rd. BN23 19 E3
Rowan Av. BN22 11 F6
Rowsley Rd. BN20 20 C6
Royal Parade. BN22 21 H2
Royal Sovereign Vw. BN23 19 G5
Royal Sussex Cres. BN20 16 D6
Rushlake Cres. BN21 17 F5
Ruskin Rd. BN20 16 D2
Rusper Rd. BN20 16 D5
Russet Clo. BN26 11 F3
Rutland Clo. BN21 17 F5
Rydal Way. BN23 12 D3
Rye Clo. BN26 11 E2
Rye St. BN22 18 D5
Ryefield Clo. BN21 17 E4
Rylstone Rd. BN22 21 H1

Sackville Rd. BN22 12 B5
Saffrons Pk. BN20 21 E4
Saffrons Rd. BN21 21 E3
St Annes Rd. BN22 10 D6
St Annes Rd. BN21 21 E1
St Anthonys Av. BN23 19 E4
St Aubyns Rd. BN22 22 D2
St Davids Clo. BN22 11 F5
St Georges Rd. BN22 22 D1
St Gregorys Clo. BN20 20 D5
St James Rd. BN22 21 H1
St Johns Dri. BN24 13 F1
St Johns Rd. BN20 20 D5
St Johns Rd. BN26 10 C3
St Lawrence Mews. BN23 19 G2
St Lawrence Pl. BN23 19 G2
St Lawrence Way. BN23 19 G2
St Leonards Pl. BN20 20 C2
St Leonards Rd. BN21 22 A2
St Leonards Ter. BN26 10 C2
St Lucia Wk. BN23 19 G3
St Martins Rd. BN22 11 F6
St Marys Clo. BN22 16 D1
St Marys Rd. BN21 20 C1
St Michaels Clo. BN24 12 C1
St Nicolas Clo. BN24 14 D3
St Pauls Clo. BN22 11 F6
St Philips Av. BN22 18 C6
St Vincents Clo. BN20 20 D4
Salehurst St. BN21 20 C2
Salisbury Clo. BN22 17 E1
Salisbury Rd. BN20 20 C5
Salvador Clo. BN23 19 G4
Sancroft Rd. BN20 20 B2
Sandown Clo. BN23 12 C3
Sandpiper Walk. BN23 13 E5
Sandwich St. BN22 18 D5
Santa Cruz Dri. BN23 19 G4
Saxby Clo. BN23 13 F6
Saxon Ground. BN21 20 D1
Saxon Pl. BN21 17 E5
Sayerland La. BN26 10 C1
Sayerland Rd. BN26 10 C1
Scanlon Clo. BN20 10 D6
Schofield Way. BN23 19 G4
School La. BN26 10 C2
Sea Rd. BN24 15 F4
Seabeach La. BN22 18 D6
Seaford Rd. BN22 18 D6
Seaside. BN22 22 D2
Seaside Rd. BN21 22 C3
Seaville Dri. BN23 19 E3
Seaville Dri. BN24 15 F4
Selby Rd. BN21 17 F6
Selmeston Rd. BN21 17 E4
Selsfield Clo. BN21 17 F5
Selwyn Dri. BN21 20 D1
Selwyn Rd. BN21 20 D1
Seven Sisters Rd. BN22 10 D6
Sevenoaks Rd. BN23 12 D5
Shakespeare Wk. BN23 13 F5
Shalfleet Clo. BN23 12 C4
Shanklin Clo. BN23 12 C3
Shannon Way. BN23 19 F3
Sheen Rd. BN22 22 D1
Sheffield Park Way. BN23 12 B3
Shelley Walk. BN23 13 F5
Shepham La. BN26 11 E2
Shepherds Clo. BN22 11 H6
Sheraton Clo. BN21 22 A4
Shinewater La. BN23 12 D3
Shipley Mill Clo. BN24 12 D2
Short Brow Clo. BN22 10 D6
Shortdean Pl. BN21 20 C1
Shortlands Clo. BN22 17 E2
Sidcup Clo. BN23 13 E5
Sidley Rd. BN22 21 H1
Silverdale Rd. BN20 21 E4
Singleton Mill Clo. BN24 12 D2
Slindon Cres. BN23 13 F6
Solomons Clo. BN23 19 H1
Snowdon Clo. BN23 13 E4
Somerville Clo. BN23 19 F4
Sorrel Clo. BN23 13 E4
Sorrel Dri. BN23 12 D4
South Av. BN20 16 D6
South Cliff. BN20 21 E5
South Cliff Av. BN20 21 F5
South Clo. BN24 15 G3
South Lynn Dri. BN21 21 E1
South St. BN21 22 A4
Southampton Clo. BN23 19 F3
Southbourne Rd. BN22 18 D5
Southdown Av. BN20 10 C6
Southdown Rd. BN20 16 D4
Southern Av. BN26 10 D3
Southern Rd. BN22 12 B5
Southfield. BN26 10 C4
Southfields Rd. BN21 21 E2
Spencer Rd. BN21 22 A4
Spring Clo. BN20 16 D2
Spring Lodge Clo. BN23 13 G5
Springfield Clo. BN24 13 G1
Springfield Rd. BN22 21 G1
Spruce Clo. BN22 17 F1
Spurway Pk. BN26 10 D4
Spur Rd. BN26 10 D4
Stables La. BN21 22 A3
Stanley Rd. BN22 21 G1
Stanmer Dri. BN22 17 E2
Stansted Rd. BN22 21 G1
Star Rd. BN21 20 D2
Station App. BN22 18 A2
Station Rd. BN26 10 C2
Station St. BN21 22 A3
Staveley Rd. BN20 20 D5
Stevenson Clo. BN23 13 F4
Stonegate Clo. BN23 12 C3
Stuart Av. BN21 17 E5
Sturdee Clo. BN23 19 G4
Sumach Clo. BN22 17 G1
Summerdown Clo. BN20 20 C3
Summerdown Rd. BN20 20 C2
Summerlands Rd. BN22 16 D1
Sunset Clo. BN24 15 G3
Sunstar La. BN26 10 A3
Susans Rd. BN21 22 B2
Sutton Rd. BN21 22 A3
Swale Clo. BN24 12 C2
Swallow Clo. BN23 12 D5
Swanley Clo. BN23 13 E5
Swinburne Av. BN22 11 E6
Sycamore Clo. BN22 11 F6
Sydney Rd. BN22 22 C1

Taddington Rd. BN22 21 H1
Tamal Clo. BN24 12 C2
Tamarack Clo. BN22 17 F1
Tanbridge Rd. BN23 13 G5
Tas Combe Dri. BN20 10 C6
Tas Combe Way. BN20 16 D2
Telscombe Rd. BN23 13 G5
Tennyson Walk. BN23 13 F4
Tenterden Clo. BN23 13 E5
Terminus Rd. BN21 22 A3
Thackeray Clo. BN23 13 F4
The Avenue. BN21 22 A2
The Beechings. BN24 15 E5
The Boulevard. BN24 15 G3
The Broadway. BN22 17 F2
The Circus. BN23 19 E3
The Cloisters. BN22 17 E1
The Close. BN20 16 D3
The Combe. BN20 16 C4
The Conifers. BN21 21 F1
The Crescent. BN20 16 D6
The Crescent, Willingdon. BN20 10 C6
The Croft. BN20 16 D2
The Crossways. BN24 12 C1
The Dene. BN20 10 C6
The Dentons. BN20 20 D5
The Goffs. BN20 20 D2
The Green Walk. BN22 11 E6
The Greys. BN20 20 D2
The Grove. BN20 10 C6
The Grove, Ratton. BN20 16 D4
The Hydneye. BN22 12 B6
The Lawns. BN22 16 D1
*The Limes, Arundel Rd. BN21 21 E2
The Millrace. BN26 10 C5
The Paddock. BN22 12 B5
The Parade. BN24 15 F4
The Paragon. BN20 10 B6
The Piazza. BN23 19 G3
The Portlands. BN23 19 G4
The Promenade. BN24 15 F5
The Quadrant. BN21 20 D1
The Rising. BN23 13 F5
The Rookery. BN23 12 D3
The Sanctuary. BN20 20 A1
The Square. BN24 15 G3
The Thatchings. BN26 10 C4
The Triangle. BN20 10 D6
The Twitten. BN24 15 E4
The Village. BN20 20 D5
The Vineries. BN23 13 F5
The Vintry. BN21 17 E4
Thornwood Clo. BN22 17 G1
Thurrock Clo. BN20 10 D6
Tidebrook Gdns. BN23 13 G5
Tideswell Rd. BN21 22 B3
Tilgate Clo. BN21 17 E4
Tillingham Clo. BN24 12 B2
Tillingham Way. BN24 12 B2
Timberlaine Rd. BN24 15 E5
Timberley Rd. BN22 17 F2
Tintern Clo. BN22 11 F6
Tolkien Rd. BN23 13 G5
Torfield Rd. BN21 21 E1
Tott Yew Rd. BN20 10 C5
Tovey Clo. BN21 17 E5
Tower Clo. BN24 15 H2
*Trafalgar Mews, Cambridge Rd. BN22 21 H2
Tremaines Rd. BN23 13 G5
Trinity Pl. BN21 22 C3
Trinity Trees. BN21 22 B4
Trossachs Clo. BN23 13 E4
Tugwell Rd. BN22 12 B4
Turner Clo. BN23 13 F6
Tutts Barn La. BN22 18 A6
Tweedsmuir Clo. BN23 13 E4
Twineham Rd. BN21 17 E4

Upland Rd. BN20 20 B3
Upper Avenue. BN21 22 B1
Upper Carlisle Rd. BN20 20 C5
Upper Dukes Dri. BN20 20 C6
Upper Kings Dri. BN20 16 D2
Upper Ratton Dri. BN20 16 C3

Upper Wish Hill. BN20 16 D3
Upperton Gdns. BN21 21 E2
Upperton La. BN21 21 E2
Upperton Rd. BN21 20 D1
Upwick Rd. BN20 20 C2

Val Prinseps Rd. BN24 15 E5
Vancouver Rd. BN23 19 H1
Ventnor Clo. BN23 12 D3
Vernon Clo. BN23 19 F4
Vian Av. BN23 19 F4
Vicarage Dri. BN20 20 C2
Vicarage La. BN20 20 C2
Vicarage Rd. BN20 20 C2
Victoria Clo. BN26 10 C2
Victoria Dri. BN20 16 D5
Victoria Gdns. BN20 20 B1
Victoria Rd. BN20 20 B1
Victoria Rd. BN26 10 C2
Viking Way. BN23 19 F3
Vincent Clo. BN23 19 G4
Vine Sq. BN22 18 D5

Wade Clo. BN23 19 F4
Wadhurst Clo. BN22 12 B5
Waldron Clo. BN22 17 E3
Walker Clo. BN23 19 F4
Wallis Av. BN23 19 E4
Wallis Pl. BN23 19 E4
Wallsend Rd. BN24 14 D3
Walnut Tree Wk. BN20 16 D3
Walnut Walk. BN26 10 C3
Walpole Walk. BN23 13 F4
Walsingham Clo. BN22 11 F6
Walton Clo. BN23 13 F4
Wannock Av. BN20 10 B6
Wannock Dri. BN26 10 C4
Wannock Gdns. BN26 10 B6
Wannock La. BN20 10 B6
Wannock Rd. BN22 18 D6
Wannock Rd. BN26 10 B5
Warburton Clo. BN21 17 F3
Warminster Rd. BN24 15 F4
Warren Clo. BN20 20 C5
Warrior Sq. BN22 21 H1
Wartling Rd. BN26 10 C4
Water Mill Clo. BN26 10 C4
Waterworks Rd. BN22 21 G1
Watts La. BN21 20 D1
Waverley Gdns. BN24 15 F4
Wayford Clo. BN23 13 E4
Wealden Park. BN22 17 E1
Weatherby Clo. BN21 17 E3
Wedderburn Rd. BN20 16 D3
Welbeck Clo. BN22 11 F6
Wellcombe Cres. BN20 20 C6
Wellesley Rd. BN21 22 C2
Wells Clo. BN20 20 B5
Wellsbourne Rd. BN24 12 C2
West Clo. BN26 10 D2
West St. BN21 22 A4
West Ter. BN21 22 A4
Westerham Rd. BN23 13 F6
Western Av. BN26 10 D3
Western Rd. BN22 21 G1
Western Rd,
  Pevensey Bay. BN24 15 F5
Westfield Clo. BN26 10 D3
Westfield Ct. BN26 10 D2
Westfield Rd. BN21 17 E5
Westham By-Pass.
  BN24 12 A1
Westham Dri. BN20 15 H3
Westlords. BN21 17 F5
Westminster Clo. BN22 11 F6
Wharf Rd. BN21 22 A2
Wheelwright Clo. BN22 11 F5
Whitbread Clo. BN23 12 D3
Whitley Rd. BN22 21 F1
Whittle Dri. BN22 12 C6
Wildwood. BN24 12 D3
Willard Clo. BN23 18 B5
Willingdon Clo. BN20 16 D2
Willingdon Ct. BN20 10 D6
Willingdon Drove.
  BN23 12 C6
Willingdon Park Dri.
  BN22 17 E1
Willingdon Rd. BN22 16 D2
Willingdon Way. BN20 16 D1
Willoughby Cres. BN22 18 B5
Willow Dri. BN26 10 C4
Willow Walk. BN22 17 E1
Willowdowne Clo.
  BN26 10 C4

Willowfield Rd. BN22 22 D1
Willowfield Sq. BN22 22 D1
Wilmington Gdns.
  BN21 22 B5
Wilmington Sq. BN21 22 B5
Wilton Av. BN22 12 B4
Winchcombe Rd. BN22 22 C1
Winchelsea Rd. BN22 18 D5
Winchester Clo. BN22 16 D1
Winchester Way. BN22 16 D1
Windermere Cres.
  BN22 18 D6
Windmill Clo. BN21 17 E5
Windmill Clo,
  Westham. BN21 13 H1
Windmill Grn. BN24 12 D2
Windmill Pl. BN26 10 C5
Windmill Rd. BN26 10 D4
Windover Way. BN26 10 D6
Windsor Clo. BN23 12 D4
Windsor Way. BN26 10 C2
Windward Quay. BN23 19 G3
Winkney Rd. BN22 12 B4
Winston Cres. BN23 19 E4
Wish Hill. BN20 16 D2
Wish Rd. BN21 22 B4
Withylam Clo. BN26 12 B5
Woburn Way. BN22 11 F6
Woodcroft Dri. BN21 17 E4
Woodgate Rd. BN22 18 C6
Woodland Av. BN22 17 E3
Woodpecker Rd. BN23 12 D5
Woodward Clo. BN23 19 F4
Wordsworth Dri. BN23 13 F5
Wrestwood Av. BN22 17 E2
Wrotham Clo. BN23 13 E5
Wroxham Rd. BN23 12 D3

Yielding Clo. BN21 17 F6
York Rd. BN21 22 A4

HAILSHAM

Acorn Grn. BN27 8 D4
Amberstone Vw. BN27 8 E3
Anglesey Av. BN27 8 C4
Antares Path. BN27 9 F6
Apex Park. BN27 9 C6
Apex Way. BN27 9 C6
Archery Walk. BN27 9 E7
Arlington Rd East. BN27 9 C7
Arlington Rd West.
  BN27 9 A7
Arran Clo. BN27 8 E3
Arundel Clo. BN27 8 E3
Ash Ct. BN27 9 C6
Ash Path. BN27 8 E3
Ashburnham Pl. BN27 8 C3
Ashford Clo. BN27 9 E6
Ashley Gdns. BN27 8 E3
Barn Clo. BN27 8 E4
Battle Cres. BN27 9 D5
Battle Rd. BN27 9 D5
Bayham Rd. BN27 9 E6
Beckenham Clo. BN27 8 D3
Beechwood Clo. BN27 9 E8
Bell Banks Rd. BN27 9 E6
Beuzeville Av. BN27 9 D5
Bexley Clo. BN27 8 D4
Birch Way. BN27 9 D7
*Bittern Ct,
  Bayham Rd. BN27 9 E6
Blacksmith Copse. BN27 9 C7
Blossom Walk. BN27 8 D4
Bowley Rd. BN27 9 E7
Bramble Dri. BN27 9 C6
*Burton Walk,
  Lindfield Dri. BN27 9 D7
Bushyfields. BN27 9 C6
Butts Field. BN27 9 E7
Caburn Way. BN27 9 C7
Cacklebury Clo. BN27 9 C7
Cameron Clo. BN27 9 C5
Capella Path. BN27 9 F6
Carpenters Way. BN27 9 C7
Carriers Path. BN27 9 D6
Chapel Barn Clo. BN27 9 E6
Cherryside. BN27 9 C6
Chestnut Clo. BN27 8 C4
Church La. BN27 8 C1
Clyde Park. BN27 9 E6
Coldthorn La. BN27 9 D8
Compton Ter. BN27 9 E7

Coopers Way. BN27 9 C7
Cornfield Grn. BN27 8 E4
Croft Woods. BN27 9 D6
Cromer Way. BN27 8 C4
Cuckoo Walk. BN27 8 D4
*Curlew Ct,
  Observatory Vw. BN27 9 F6
Dacre Park. BN27 9 F6
Danum Clo. BN27 9 F6
Derwent Clo. BN27 9 C5
Diplocks Way. BN27 9 C6
Ditchling Way. BN27 9 D7
Douglas Clo. BN27 8 C4
Downs View Way. BN27 9 D6
Dunbar Dri. BN27 8 C4
Eastwell Pl. BN27 9 D5
Elizabeth Ct. BN27 9 E6
Elm Grn. BN27 8 D4
Elmsdown Pl. BN27 9 E6
Ersham Rd. BN27 9 D8
Ersham Way. BN27 9 D7
Factory La. BN27 9 C7
Fair Isle Clo. BN27 8 C4
Falcon Way. BN27 8 D3
Farmland Way. BN27 8 E4
Farne Clo. BN27 8 B4
Fern Grn. BN27 8 D4
*Fieldfare Ct,
  Greenwich Rd. BN27 9 F6
Fir Tree Clo. BN27 9 E6
Forest View. BN27 9 C5
Freshfield Clo. BN27 9 D7
Garfield Rd. BN27 9 D6
Geering Pk. BN27 9 F6
Gemma Clo. BN27 9 F6
George St. BN27 9 D6
Gilbert Way. BN27 9 D8
Gleneagles Dri. BN27 9 B6
Goodwin Clo. BN27 8 B4
Gordon Rd. BN27 9 D7
Green Gro. BN27 9 D6
Green Walk. BN27 8 E4
Greenacres Dri. BN27 9 E6
Greenacres Way. BN27 9 E6
Greenfields. BN27 8 C4
Greenwich Rd. BN27 9 F6
Grovelands Rd. BN27 9 C5
Hailsham By-Pass.
  BN27 8 A3
Hailsham Ind Park.
  BN27 9 C6
Hailsham Rd. BN27 9 D8
Halley Pk. BN27 9 F6
Hamelsham Ct. BN27 9 C6
Hanover Ct. BN27 8 E3
Harebeating Clo. BN27 8 E3
Harebeating Cres. BN27 8 D3
Harebeating Dri. BN27 8 D3
Harebeating Gdns. BN27 8 E3
Harebeating La. BN27 8 E4
Harmers Hay Rd. BN27 8 D4
*Harriers Ct,
  Bayham Rd. BN27 9 E6
Hawkins Way. BN27 9 D6
Hawks Farm Clo. BN27 8 D3
Hawks Rd. BN27 8 D4
Hawkstown Cres. BN27 8 D3
Hawkstown Gdns. BN27 8 D3
Hawkstown View. BN27 8 E3
Hawkswood Dri. BN27 8 E3
Hawkswood Rd. BN27 8 D4
Hawthylands Cres. BN27 8 D3
Hawthylands Dri. BN27 8 D3
Hawthylands Rd. BN27 8 D4
Hayland Grn. BN27 8 E4
Hempstead La. BN27 8 B4
*Heron Ct,
  Bayham Rd. BN27 9 E6
High St. BN27 9 D5
Hollamby Pk. BN27 9 F6
Holly Clo. BN27 9 D8
*Holywell Walk,
  Lindfield Dri. BN27 9 D7
Honeysuckle Clo. BN27 9 C7
Howard Clo. BN27 9 F7
Howletts Dri. BN27 8 D4
Ilex Grn. BN27 8 D4
INDUSTRIAL & RETAIL:
Apex Park. BN27 9 C7
Hailsham Ind Park.
  BN27 9 C6
Station Rd Ind Est.
  BN27 9 E7
Swan Farm Business
  Centre. BN27 9 F7

Ingrams Way. BN27 9 C8
Iona Clo. BN27 8 C3
Jasmine Grn. BN27 8 D4
*Kestrel Ct,
  Greenwich Rd. BN27 9 F6
*Kingfisher Ct,
  Greenwich Rd. BN27 9 F6
Knights Gdn. BN27 9 D7
Laburnam Grn. BN27 8 D4
Landsdowne Cres. BN27 8 D3
Landsdowne Rd. BN27 8 C3
Landsdowne Way. BN27 8 C3
Lansdowne Dri. BN27 8 C3
Lansdowne Gdns. BN27 8 D3
*Lapwing Ct,
  Bayham Rd. BN27 9 E6
*Leamland Walk,
  Lindfield Dri. BN27 9 D7
Lepelands. BN27 8 C4
Linden Gro. BN27 8 E3
Lindfield Dri. BN27 9 D6
Little Marshfoot La.
  BN27 9 F7
London Rd. BN27 8 C3
Lower Horsebridge Rd.
  BN27 8 A3
*Luke Lade Ct,
  Bayham Rd. BN27 9 E6
Lundy Wk. BN27 8 C3
Magham Rd. BN27 8 E3
Manor Park Clo. BN27 8 C3
Manor Park Rd. BN27 8 C3
Maple Ct. BN27 9 C6
Mare Bay Clo. BN27 8 C3
Market Pl. BN27 9 E6
Market Sq. BN27 9 E6
Market St. BN27 9 E6
Marshfoot La. BN27 9 E6
Meadow Clo. BN27 9 D5
Meadow Rd. BN27 9 C7
Medway. BN27 8 C4
Melrose Clo. BN27 9 C5
*Merlin Ct,
  Observatory Vw. BN27 9 F6
Mill La. BN27 8 C1
Mill Rd. BN27 9 E6
Milland Mews. BN27 8 D4
Milland Rd. BN27 8 D4
Millers Rise. BN27 9 C7
Moore Pk. BN27 9 F6
Moray Wk. BN27 8 C4
Mortain Pk. BN27 9 F6
Mount View Ter. BN27 9 E7
Mountain Ash Clo.
  BN27 9 C5
New Barn Clo. BN27 9 E7
New Rd. BN27 9 D1
Newton Pk. BN27 9 F6
North Heath Clo. BN27 8 E4
North St,
  Hailsham. BN27 9 D6
North St, Lower
  Horsebridge. BN27 8 B1
Nursery Clo. BN27 9 E6
Nursery Path. BN27 9 D7
Oaklands Way. BN27 9 C7
Oaktree Way. BN27 8 E4
Observatory Vw. BN27 9 F6
Old Mill Clo. BN27 8 C3
Old Orchard Pl. BN27 9 D6
Old Swan La. BN27 9 F8
Oldfield Cres. BN27 8 D4
Orion Clo. BN27 9 F6
Otham Pk. BN27 9 F6
Park Clo. BN27 9 D7
Park Gate. BN27 8 F3
Park Rd. BN27 8 D1
Paul Clo. BN27 8 C3
Pelham Cres. BN27 9 E7
Pembroke Clo. BN27 8 E3
Phoenix Clo. BN27 9 F6
Pine Way. BN27 9 C6
Pitreavie Dri. BN27 9 C5
*Plover Ct,
  Observatory Vw. BN27 9 F6
Polegate Rd. BN27 9 E6
Portland Clo. BN27 8 C4
*Quail Ct,
  Observatory Vw. BN27 9 F6
Quinnell Dri. BN27 8 D3
Quintin Clo. BN27 9 C8
*Redshank Ct,
  Observatory Vw. BN27 9 F6
Robin Post La. BN27 9 B8
Rockall Dri. BN27 8 C3
Rope Walk. BN27 9 D5

Sackville Rd. BN27 9 E7
St Andrews Clo. BN27 8 C4
St Boswells Clo. BN27 9 B5
St Marys Av. BN27 9 E6
St Marys Walk. BN27 9 E6
St. Mellion.Clo. BN27 9 B5
St Wilfreds Dri. BN27 9 D5
Sandbanks Clo. BN27 9 D7
Sandbanks Gdns. BN27 9 D8
Sandbanks Gro. BN27 9 D8
Sandbanks Rd. BN27 9 C7
Sandbanks Way. BN27 9 D7
Sheppey Walk. BN27 8 C3
Sherwood Grn. BN27 9 D7
Silverdale Clo. BN27 9 D5
Solway. BN27 8 C4
South Clo. BN27 9 D7
South Rd. BN27 9 C7
Southerden Clo. BN27 9 E6
Station Rd Ind Est.
  BN27 9 E7
Station Rd. BN27 9 D6
Station Rd,
  Hellingly. BN27 8 C1
Stony La. BN27 9 E6
Stroma Gdns. BN27 8 C3
Sturton Pl. BN27 9 D6
Summer Ct. BN27 9 D7
Summerfield Av. BN27 9 D5
Summerheath Rd. BN27 9 D5
Sunningdale Ct. BN27 8 C4
Sussex Av. BN27 9 C5
Sussex Clo. BN27 9 D6
Swan Farm
  Business Centre. BN27 9 F7
Swan Rd. BN27 9 E7
Sycamore Dri. BN27 9 D8
*Teal Ct,
  Observatory Vw. BN27 9 F6
Tennis Clo. BN27 9 D6
The Avenue. BN27 9 D7
The Belfry. BN27 9 B6
The Cedars. BN27 8 D4
The Diplocks. BN27 9 C6
The Drive. BN27 9 D7
The Gages. BN27 9 F6
The Glade. BN27 9 B7
The Green. BN27 8 E3
The Grove. BN27 9 D7
The Hawthorns. BN27 9 C6
The Holt. BN27 9 C7
The Lowlands. BN27 8 C4
The Mount. BN27 9 E7
The Paddocks. BN27 8 C3
The Quentins. BN27 9 E6
The Stiles. BN27 9 E6
The Stringwalk. BN27 9 E7
Tilehurst Clo. BN27 9 C5
Timber Ct. BN27 9 E6
Turnberry Dri. BN27 9 B6
Union Clo. BN27 8 D4
Upper Horsebridge Rd.
  BN27 8 C3
Vega Clo. BN27 9 F6
Vicarage Field. BN27 9 E6
Vicarage La. BN27 9 E5
*Vicarage Mews,
  Vicarage Rd. BN27 9 E6
Vicarage Rd. BN27 9 E6
Victoria Rd. BN27 9 E6
Warwick Clo. BN27 8 E3
Wentworth Clo. BN27 8 B4
Western Rd. BN27 9 C5
Whiffens Clo. BN27 9 C7
Willow Av. BN27 8 D4
Windsor Rd. BN27 9 D7
Woburn Clo. BN27 8 C4
Woodland Clo. BN27 8 E4
Woodpecker Dr. BN27 9 C5

LEWES

Abergavenny Rd. BN7 4 C3
Abinger Pl. BN7 5 E3
Albion St. BN7 5 E3
Annes Path. BN7 4 D5
Antioch St. BN7 4 D4
Arundel Green. BN7 4 D2
Barn Hatch Clo. BN7 4 B5
Barn Rd. BN7 5 F1
Barons Walk. BN7 4 B4
Barons Down Rd. BN7 4 B5
Baxter Rd. BN7 4 C2

Beckett Way. BN7 5 E1
Bell La. BN7 4 C5
Berkeley Row. BN7 4 C5
Bishop Dri. BN7 4 B4
Blois Rd. BN7 4 B1
Boughey Pl. BN7 5 E1
Bradford Rd. BN7 4 D4
Bridgewick Clo. BN7 5 E1
Brighton Rd. BN7 4 A5
Brook St. BN7 5 E3
Brooks Clo. BN7 5 F2
Brooks La. BN7 5 F3
Brooks Rd. BN7 5 F2
Broomans La. BN7 5 E4
Buckhurst Clo. BN7 5 E1
Buckwell Ct. BN7 4 B1
Bull La. BN7 5 E4
Caburn Cres. BN7 4 B2
Castle Banks. BN7 5 E4
Castle Ditch La. BN7 5 E4
Castle Gate. BN7 5 E4
Castle Precincts. BN7 5 E4
Chapel Hill. BN7 5 G3
Christie Rd. BN7 4 C3
Church La, Lewes. BN7 4 D4
Church La,
South Malling. BN7 5 E2
Church Row. BN7 5 E3
Church Twitten. BN7 5 E4
Churchill Rd. BN7 4 C1
Clare Rd. BN7 4 C2
Cleve Ter. BN7 4 D5
Cliffe High St. BN7 5 F3
Cluny Clo. BN7 4 D5
Cluny St. BN7 4 D5
Cockshut Rd. BN7 4 D5
Coombe Rd. BN7 5 F2
Court Rd. BN7 5 F4
Cranedown. BN7 4 C6
Cranmer Clo. BN7 5 F2
Crisp Rd. BN7 4 C1
Cross Way. BN7 4 B3
Dale Rd. BN7 4 C5
Daveys La. BN7 5 F3
De Grey Clo. BN7 5 F2
De Montfort Rd. BN7 4 C4
De Warrenne Rd. BN7 4 C3
Deanery Clo. BN7 5 F1
Delaware Rd. BN7 4 B5
Dorset Rd. BN7 5 E5
Downs Clo. BN7 4 B2
Downside. BN7 4 B4
Dunvan Clo. BN7 5 E1
Earls Gdns. BN7 5 E3
East St. BN7 5 E3
Eastgate St. BN7 5 F3
Eastgate Wharf. BN7 5 F3
Eastport La. BN7 5 E5
Eastway. BN7 4 A2
Edward St. BN7 5 E3
Eleanor Clo. BN7 4 D3
Elm Gro. BN7 5 E4
Englishs Passage. BN7 5 F3
Eridge Green. BN7 4 C2
Evelyn Rd. BN7 4 C2
Farncombe Rd. BN7 5 F4
Ferrers Rd. BN7 4 C3
Firle Cres. BN7 4 A2
Fisher St. BN7 5 E3
Fitzgerald Rd. BN7 5 F1
Fitzjohn Rd. BN7 4 C3
Fitzroy Rd. BN7 4 C1
Foundry La. BN7 5 F4
Friars Walk. BN7 5 F4
Fuller Rd. BN7 4 C1
Garden St. BN7 5 E4
Glebe Clo. BN7 4 B5
Godfrey Clo. BN7 5 E1
Grange Rd. BN7 4 D5
Green La. BN7 5 E4
Green Wall. BN7 5 F3
Greyfriars Ct. BN7 5 F4
Gundreda Rd. BN7 4 C2
Ham La. BN7 5 F5
Hamsey Cres. BN7 4 B2
Harvard Clo. BN7 5 E1
Harveys Way. BN7 5 F3
Hawkenbury Way. BN7 4 B3
Hayward Rd. BN7 4 C1
Hereward Way. BN7 5 F2
High St. BN7 4 D4
Highdown Rd. BN7 4 B2
Hill Rd. BN7 4 B2
Hillman Clo. BN7 5 G4
Hillyfield. BN7 4 C5
Hoopers Clo. BN7 5 E1
Horsfield Rd. BN7 4 C1
Houndean Clo. BN7 4 B4
Houndean Rise. BN7 4 A5
INDUSTRIAL & RETAIL:
Cliffe Ind Est. BN7 5 H5
Malling Brook Ind Est.
BN7 5 F2
Phoenix Ind Est. BN7 5 E3
Irelands La. BN7 4 D4
Juggs Clo. BN7 4 C5
Juggs Rd. BN7 4 A6
Keere St. BN7 4 D4
King Henrys Rd. BN7 4 C2
Kingsley Rd. BN7 4 C2
Kingston Rd. BN7 4 C6
Lambert Pl. BN7 5 E1
Lancaster St. BN7 5 E3
Landport Rd. BN7 4 C1
Lansdown Pl. BN7 5 E4
Lee Rd. BN7 4 C2
Leicester Rd. BN7 4 C3
Lewes Southern
By-Pass. BN7 4 A6
Little East St. BN7 5 E3
Lodge Clo. BN7 4 B4
Love Lane. BN7 4 B5
Malling Clo. BN7 5 F1
Malling Down. BN7 5 F1
Malling Hill. BN7 5 F1
Malling St. BN7 5 G3
Mantell Clo. BN7 5 E1
Market La. BN7 5 E4
Market St. BN7 5 E4
Mayhew Way. BN7 5 E2
Mealla Cl. BN7 5 E1
Meridian Rd. BN7 4 C2
Middle Way. BN7 4 B3
Mildmay Rd. BN7 4 C3
Mill Rd. BN7 5 F1
Monks La. BN7 4 D5
Monks Way. BN7 5 E1
Montacute Rd. BN7 4 A5
Morley Clo. BN7 4 D5
Morris Rd. BN7 5 F4
Mount Harry Rd. BN7 4 B2
Mount Pl. BN7 5 E4
Mount Pleasant. BN7 5 E3
Mount St. BN7 5 E5
Mountfield Rd. BN7 5 E5
Nevill Cres. BN7 4 B3
Nevill Rd. BN7 4 B2
New Rd. BN7 5 E4
Newton Rd. BN7 4 D2
North Ct. BN7 5 F3
North St. BN7 5 E3
North Way. BN7 4 B3
Offham Rd. BN7 4 B1
Old Malling Way. BN7 5 E1
Orchard Rd. BN7 5 G2
Ousedale Clo. BN7 4 C4
Paddock La. BN7 4 D4
Paddock Rd. BN7 4 D4
Paines Twitten. BN7 5 E4
Park Rd. BN7 4 D3
Peckham Clo. BN7 5 E1
Pelham Ter. BN7 5 E3
Pellbrook Rd. BN7 4 C1
Phoenix Causeway. BN7 5 F3
Phoenix Pl. BN7 5 E3
Pinwell Rd. BN7 5 E4
Pipe Passage. BN7 4 D4
Potters La. BN7 4 D5
Prince Charles Rd. BN7 5 F1
Prince Edwards Rd. BN7 4 C3
Priory Court. BN7 5 E5
Priory Cres. BN7 5 E5
Priory St. BN7 5 E5
Queen Annes Clo. BN7 4 D3
Queens Rd. BN7 5 F1
Railway La. BN7 5 F4
Riverdale. BN7 5 E2
Rotten Row. BN7 4 D4
Rufus Clo. BN7 4 D3
Russell Row. BN7 5 E1
Sackville Clo. BN7 4 D3
St Andrews La. BN7 5 E4
St Annes Cres. BN7 4 C4
St James St. BN7 4 D5
St Johns Hill. BN7 5 E3
St Johns St. BN7 5 E3
St Johns Ter. BN7 5 E3
St Martins La. BN7 5 E4
St Michaels Ter. BN7 5 E2
St Nicholas La. BN7 5 E4
St Pancras Gdns. BN7 4 D5
St Pancras Rd. BN7 4 D5
St Peters Pl. BN7 4 D4
St Swithuns La. BN7 5 E4
St Swithuns Ter. BN7 5 E4
School Hill. BN7 5 E4
Segrave Clo. BN7 4 C3
Sheep Fair. BN7 4 B2
Shelley Clo. BN7 4 C3
South Downs Rd. BN7 5 F2
South St. BN7 5 G4
South Way. BN7 4 B3
Southcliffe. BN7 5 G4
Southdown Av. BN7 4 B4
Southdown Pl. BN7 5 G3
Southover High St. BN7 4 D5
Southover Rd. BN7 5 E4
Spences Field. BN7 5 F2
Spences La. BN7 5 F2
Spital Clo. BN7 4 C4
Spital Rd. BN7 4 C4
Spring Gdns. BN7 5 E3
Stansfield Rd. BN7 4 D2
Station Rd. BN7 5 E5
Station St. BN7 5 E4
Stewards Inn. BN7 5 E4
Stoneham Clo. BN7 5 E1
Sun St. BN7 5 E3
Talbot Ter. BN7 5 E3
Tanners Brook. BN7 5 E4
The Avenue. BN7 4 D3
The Course. BN7 4 D5
The Gallops. BN7 4 B4
The Lynchets. BN7 5 G1
The Martlets. BN7 5 F1
The Meadows. BN7 5 F1
The Spinneys. BN7 5 G2
Thomas St. BN7 5 G3
Timber Yd Cotts. BN7 5 G4
Toronto Ter. BN7 5 E3
Ty La. BN7 5 G4
Valence Rd. BN7 4 C3
Valley Rd. BN7 4 C5
Verralls Walk. BN7 4 D5
Waite Clo. BN7 5 F2
Waldshut Rd. BN7 4 B1
Wallands Cres. BN7 4 D3
Walwers La. BN7 5 E4
Warren Clo. BN7 4 C4
Warren Dri. BN7 4 C4
Watergate La. BN7 5 E4
Waterloo Pl. BN7 5 E3
Weald Clo. BN7 4 D3
Wellhouse Pl. BN7 4 D4
Wellington St. BN7 5 E3
West St. BN7 5 E3
Western Rd. BN7 4 C4
Westgate St. BN7 4 D4
Wheatsheaf Gdns. BN7 5 G3
White Hill. BN7 4 D3
Windover Cres. BN7 4 B2
Winterbourne Clo. BN7 4 B5
Winterbourne Hollow.
BN7 4 C4
Winterbourne La. BN7 4 B5
Winterbourne Mews.
BN7 4 C5

SEAFORD

Adelaide Clo. BN25 6 C2
Albany Rd. BN25 6 B4
Alexandra Clo. BN25 6 C2
Alfriston Pk. BN25 7 H2
Alfriston Rd. BN25 7 F3
Antony Clo. BN25 6 A1
Aquila Park. BN25 7 F4
Argent Clo. BN25 7 F2
Arundel Rd. BN25 7 F4
Ash Dri. BN25 7 H4
Ashurst Rd. BN25 7 E5
Audrey Clo. BN25 6 C2
Avondale Rd. BN25 6 D4

Badgers Copse. BN25 7 G4
Bainbridge Clo. BN25 7 E5
Balmoral Clo. BN25 7 F2
Barcombe Av. BN25 7 H5
Barcombe Clo. BN25 7 H5
Barn Clo. BN25 7 F2
Barn Rise. BN25 7 F2
Barons Clo. BN25 6 B2
Battle Clo. BN25 7 G2
Beach Clo. BN25 6 C4
Beacon Clo. BN25 6 C3
Beacon Dri. BN25 6 C3
Beacon Rd. BN25 6 C3
Beame Ct. BN25 6 C4
Belgrave Cres. BN25 7 E2
Belgrave Rd. BN25 6 C4
Belvedere Gdns. BN25 7 F2
Benenden Clo. BN25 7 F3
Berwick Clo. BN25 6 B3
Birling Clo. BN25 6 C3
Bishops Clo. BN25 6 B3
Bishopstone Rd. BN25 6 A2
Blatchington Clo. BN25 7 E3
Blatchington Hill. BN25 6 D3
Blatchington Rd. BN25 6 D4
Blue Haze Av. BN25 7 F3
Bodiam Clo. BN25 7 G3
Bowden Rise. BN25 6 D2
Bracken Rd. BN25 7 F5
Bramber Clo. BN25 7 E5
Bramber La. BN25 6 D5
Bramber Rd. BN25 7 E5
Broad St. BN25 6 D4
Bromley Rd. BN25 7 F3
Brooklyn Rd. BN25 6 D4
Buckingham Clo. BN25 6 D3
Buckland Rd. BN25 7 E3
Buckle By-Pass. BN25 6 B2
Buckle Clo. BN25 6 B3
Buckle Dri. BN25 6 B3
Buckle Rise. BN25 6 B3
Buckthorn Clo. BN25 7 G4
Bydown. BN25 7 F3

Carlton Clo. BN25 6 C3
Carlton Rd. BN25 6 C3
Caroline Clo. BN25 6 C2
Chalvington Clo. BN25 7 E1
Chapel Clo. BN25 6 D3
Charles Clo. BN25 6 C2
Chartwell Clo. BN25 6 C1
Chatham Pl. BN25 6 D5
Chesterton Av. BN25 7 G4
Chesterton Dri. BN25 7 G4
Chichester Clo. BN25 6 D4
Chichester Rd. BN25 6 D4
Church La. BN25 6 D5
Church St. BN25 6 D5
Churchill Rd. BN25 6 C2
Chyngton Av. BN25 7 G3
Chyngton Gdns. BN25 7 G3
Chyngton La. BN25 7 H4
Chyngton La Nth. BN25 7 H4
Chyngton Pl. BN25 7 F5
Chyngton Rd. BN25 7 E5
Chyngton Way. BN25 7 G5
Cinque Ports Way. BN25 7 G3
Claremont Rd. BN25 6 C4
Clementine Av. BN25 6 B2
Cliff Clo. BN25 7 E6
Cliff Gdns. BN25 7 E6
Cliff Rd. BN25 7 E6
Clinton La. BN25 6 D4
Clinton Pl. BN25 6 D4
College Rd. BN25 6 D5
Connaught Rd. BN25 6 B4
Cornfield Clo. BN25 7 E4
Cornfield Rd. BN25 7 E4
Corsica Clo. BN25 7 E6
Corsica Rd. BN25 7 E6
Cradle Hill Rd. BN25 7 F2
Cricketfield Rd. BN25 6 D5
Crooked La. BN25 6 D5
Crouch La. BN25 6 D5
Crown Hill. BN25 6 D1
Cuckmere Rd. BN25 7 F5

Dane Clo. BN25 6 C5
Dane Rd. BN25 6 C5
Darwall Dri. BN25 7 F5
Deal Av. BN25 7 G2
Dean Rd. BN25 7 E5
Dover Clo. BN25 7 H2
Downs Rd. BN25 7 F4
Downsview Rd. BN25 7 E4
Duchess Dri. BN25 6 D1
Dukes Clo. BN25 6 C2
Dulwich Clo. BN25 7 F3
Dymchurch Clo. BN25 7 G3
Dymock Clo. BN25 7 H3

Earls Clo. BN25 6 B2
East Albany Rd. BN25 7 E4
East Dean Rise. BN25 7 F3
East St. BN25 6 D5
Eastbourne Rd. BN25 7 F4
Edinburgh Rd. BN25 6 C4
Edward Clo. BN25 6 A1
Eleanor Clo. BN25 6 C2
Elgin Gdns. BN25 7 H4
Elm Clo. BN25 7 H4
Esher Clo. BN25 7 E3
Esplanade. BN25 6 D5
Esplanade Mews. BN25 6 D5
Etherton Way. BN25 7 F3
Eton Clo. BN25 7 F3

Fairways Clo. BN25 7 G5
Fairways Rd. BN25 7 G5
Farm Clo. BN25 7 G3
Field Clo. BN25 7 G5
Findon Clo. BN25 7 H5
Firle Clo. BN25 6 D3
Firle Dri. BN25 6 D2
Firle Grange. BN25 6 D2
Firle Rd. BN25 6 D2
Fitzgerald Av. BN25 7 E5
Fitzgerald Park. BN25 7 E5
Flint Clo. BN25 6 D1
Folkestone Clo. BN25 7 G2
Foster Clo. BN25 6 D3
Freeland Clo. BN25 6 A1
Friston Clo. BN25 6 B3

Gerald Rd. BN25 7 E6
Gildredge Rd. BN25 7 E4
Glebe Dri. BN25 6 D4
Grand Avenue. BN25 6 B2
Green La. BN25 6 D5
Green Walk. BN25 7 F5
Greenwell Clo. BN25 7 G3
Grosvenor Rd. BN25 6 C4
Grove Rd. BN25 6 D4
Guardswell Pl. BN25 6 D4

Hamsey La. BN25 7 H5
Hanover Clo. BN25 6 A1
Harbour View Clo. BN25 6 A1
Harrison Rd. BN25 7 F3
Harrow Clo. BN25 7 F3
Hartfield Rd. BN25 7 E4
Hastings Av. BN25 7 G2
Haven Brow. BN25 7 F3
Hawth Clo. BN25 6 B3
Hawth Cres. BN25 6 B3
Hawth Gro. BN25 6 B3
Hawth Hill. BN25 6 B3
Hawth Park Rd. BN25 6 B3
Hawth Pl. BN25 6 B3
Hawth Rise. BN25 6 B3
Hawth Way. BN25 6 C4
Hazeldene. BN25 7 F4
Headland Av. BN25 7 E5
Heathfield Rd. BN25 7 E5
High St. BN25 6 D5
Highlands Rd. BN25 7 E4
Hill Rise. BN25 6 B2
Hillside Av. BN25 7 G2
Hindover Cres. BN25 7 F4
Hindover Rd. BN25 7 F3
Holters Way. BN25 6 D2
Homefield Clo. BN25 6 D3
Homefield Rd. BN25 6 D3
Hurdis Rd. BN25 6 A1
Hythe Clo. BN25 7 H3
Hythe Cres. BN25 7 G3
Hythe View. BN25 7 H3

INDUSTRIAL & RETAIL:
Cradle Hill Ind Est.
BN25 7 G2
Isabel Clo. BN25 6 C2

Jevington Dri. BN25 6 B3
Jubilee Gdns. BN25 7 E2
Juniper Clo. BN25 7 G4

Kammond Av. BN25 7 G2
Katherine Way. BN25 6 C2
Kedale Rd. BN25 6 D3
Kimberley Rd. BN25 6 B4
Kings Ride. BN25 6 C3
Kingsmead. BN25 6 C3
Kingsmead Clo. BN25 6 D3
Kingsmead La. BN25 6 C3
Kingsmead Walk. BN25 6 D3
Kingsmead Way. BN25 6 D3
Kingston Av. BN25 7 G4
Kingston Clo. BN25 7 G5
Kingston Green. BN25 7 G4
Kingston Way. BN25 7 G5
Kingsway. BN25 6 C3